VOICELESS VOICES

Words From a Broken Heart & Renewed Soul

VOICELESS VOICES: Words from a Broken Heart & Renewed Soul

Publisher page

VOICELESS VOICES

Words From a Broken Heart & Renewed Soul

Khalilah H. Purnell

Voiceless Voices Copyright @2022 Khalilah H. Purnell

Editing Services provided by B.D.G

Cover Illustration by B.D.G

All rights reserved under American Copyright Conventions.

No parts of this book may be reproduced, scanned, downloaded, decompiled, stored in a retrieval system, or transformed in any form or by any means, electronic, mechanical, photocopying, recording, or otherwise, without the prior written permission of the author. Piracy of copyrighted material is a criminal offense. Purchase only authorized editions.

Voiceless Voices: Words from A Broken Heart and Renewed Soul

Khalilah H. Purnell, Newport News, VA. 2022

Library of Congress Cataloging-in-Publication Data

Purnell, Khalilah

ISBN-13

978-0-578-29506-0

Printed in the United States of America

Dedication

I dedicate this book to my only child, my daughter, Asonte' Monique Purnell, you are one of my greatest motivations in "LIFE" and my reason WHY.

Also, I dedicate this book to my father, the late Floyd H. Bishop Jr. May he continue to rest peacefully.

To my first cousin Zenelia Bishop, who I grew up with as a sister, who lost her life at the age of 30 to senseless gun violence, her story was part of the inspiration and words in this book. To my only uncle, the late Andre' K. Purnell.

I also dedicate this book to my brother Phil, who has been in and out of the system since the age of twelve and was wrongly convicted of a crime he did not commit, yet he was charged and convicted without evidence, and it has destroyed parts of his being and life, well into adulthood, and to his wife, my sis in love, Taya Bishop, I pray some of the words on these pages help your healing journey too.

Lastly, I dedicate this book to all of you who have been affected by the traumas of this world, which have gone unhealed and unresolved. Many still endure such traumas and have no clue as to how they will get through it, or even if they will be able to. So many of you have no clue on how to finally breathe again after the pain, but this book is dedicated to you in hopes of giving you your voice back, as well as the will to see that you can, and you will get through, and your healing can start as you read the words on these pages from the heart. There is a poem for every situation. Go on and exhale now, Kings and Queens, victory, strength, healing, Power, and Renewal is yours.

VOICELESS VOICES: Words from a Broken Heart & Renewed Soul

Acknowledgements

The late DMX said to "Turn your pain into words." That is exactly what I did with this book. I turned my pains and the pains of this world that I carry on my shoulders into words.

GOD! I thank you for trusting me with this assignment. I understood the purpose.

CONTENTS

Acknowledgement pg. 7

Section 1: Concealed Truths pg. 12

BACK IN SOCIETY **pg. 19**

2 MY KINGS BEHIND BARS **pg. 16**

DISARM THE VIOLENCE   **pg. 21**

EQUAL STANDARDS   **pg. 27**

OUR LIVES MATTER TOO   **pg. 34**

MISCARRIAGE OF JUSTICE **pg. 40**

POWER OF HATE   **pg. 47**

RACISM WITH A TWIST   **pg. 50**

NEW N.I.G.G.A MENTALITY   **pg. 57**

THEY PREY   **pg. 61**

WE REPRESENT STRENGTH pg. 64

NO LONGER A DREAM   pg. 71

VOICELESS SOLITUDE   pg. 77

PROUD TO BE ME (I'M GAY)   pg. 87

UNHEALED   pg. 91

INNOCENCE LOST   pg. 97

THE PAINS I HIDE   pg. 102

THE LESSON   pg.106

THEY DESTROYED ME   pg. 111

HELL OF A MASTER   pg. 117

LIFE FOREVER CHANGED pg. 121

EXHAUSTED BLACK WOMAN   pg. 126

BROKEN   pg. 127

CAN YOU SEE ME?   pg. 130

COMPLETELY TIRED   pg. 134

DADDY   pg. 137

FACE OF THE DEVIL **pg. 139**

FEELINGS OF ANGER   pg. 142

HATEFUL RAGE   pg. 145

HAVE YOU EVER?   pg. 149

INFIDELITY   pg. 152

LIFE pg. 155

MISTREATED pg. 158

MY CLOSURE 163

NO TOLERANCE pg. 166

OVER & DONE pg.169

PAINFUL EYES pg. 171

PATTERN OF LOVE pg. 175

STILL IN LOVE pg. 179

WITHOUT REMORSE pg. 182

WOMAN FED UP pg. 189

WOMAN SCORNED pg. 192

SOUL RENEWED pg. 196

A WOMAN'S WORTH pg. 198

BROTHER pg. 201

CONNECTED FOREVER pg. 205

FINDING YOURSELF pg. 209

I WANT TO KNOW YOU pg. 214

LIVE LIFE pg. 217

MY ANGEL NOW pg. 220

SOUL RENEWED pg. 222

SPIRITUAL SOLITUDE pg. 226

THE PRESENCE OF GOD   pg. 229

TRUE FRIEND   pg. 233

WHAT IT MEANS TO LOVE   pg. 237

WHEN I LOOK AT YOU   pg. 239

YOU   pg. 245

Thank You pg. 249

Contact Page   pg. 253

VOICELESS VOICES: Words from a Broken Heart & Renewed Soul

VOICELESS VOICES: Words from a Broken Heart & Renewed Soul

SECTION I: Concealed Truths

"I pray each day, that I do not stand in my own way, so that I can do what I have been created to do. I keep remembering it isn't just about me. Its about who I touch".

Lisa Nichols

VOICELESS VOICES: Words from a Broken Heart & Renewed Soul

2 MY KINGS BEHIND BARS

You are down, I get it, you are doing time.

For a crime that you may or may not have committed

But realize who you are my brother,

You are, divine by design, A king slowed down for a little time.

But be wise with your time.

See King, the bars around you are there to break you down and keep you stagnant.

But your intelligence is the way to become free,

Do not allow them to break you down mentally.

My purpose is to empower, uplift, speak up for, save lives, and of course, teach,

My passion is in my voice and knowing I made a difference.

Because I know that there are too many lives for me to reach.

Brother, you are a king, you must see it for what it is.

You cannot allow yourself to be controlled by your current situation,

Use this time to learn and enlighten those around you.

Your minds together will free you from the agenda of

The system's mass incarceration.

I know, it is easier said than done.

But this system of bars is made to make you believe that no one cares,

They want you to give up on your life or think there is no better way.

While pushing you to lose your mind and yourself while you are in there.

You are a strong man with intelligence.

Laced with strength and a purpose,

Your present situation does not define you.

Make your plans and visualize the victory for when you touch outside, stand firm on your ambitions, and stay focused.

Use the books in there.

As medicine for your pain,

Use what I am giving you to help others.

And use your mistakes to be band-aids for those stains.

Do not allow the disease called bars and guards.

To poison your mind,

Although at times you will feel all that you feel

Is inadequate at times.

Take this time to reflect and find the truth in you,

Take the knowledge that I am giving you in my letters.

To enlighten and inspire another king too.

So, King, I am going to end this letter here.

Just remember to continue to visualize the realities of your vision,

I have given you the blueprint, it is up to you now to elevate it.

Only you can choose what to do with the rest of your time, it is your decision.

One last thing, be mindful my brother.

And when you touch out leave that mentality behind, but be mindful of what others may say,

Know what to retain, but also know what to throw away.

BACK IN SOCIETY

Walking out of these walls of slavery

For all these years, the only home many of us has known,

Will society or my family welcome me back with open arms

Or will I be forced to walk through life alone?

I am ready to change all my ways but

Will I be able to get a job to live and get by?

Will there be any opportunities or second chances?

For someone, such as I?

Soon these gates will open, and I will be set Free

But I constantly wonder what is out there in the world for me.

Anything that you take from me, it can be given back

Accept my loved ones through death and time,

I was enraged in that cage but now I am free

And now the fears of life are consuming my mind.

Will I be able to live in society?

Will it be easy for me to cope?

Or will I be lost altogether trying to learn how to live outside of here

And fall into a depression from losing all my hope?

I promised myself that I would never return

Or be put in a position to ever have to come back.

I feel lost already and I have yet to leave from behind the gate,

To step back into society, a world I doubt I will be able to relate.

DISARM THE VIOLENCE

I have three words for you: SENSELESS GUN VIOLENCE!

Has this phrase destroyed any parts of your family?

Gun Violence in the African American Community seems so natural.

Have you heard this phrase before, has it taken a loved one from you?

Why does no one want to speak on the severity of this issue plaguing and destroying us, but loud when it is an officer or another race behind killing us?

How can we gain the power we need to fight them, if we refuse to stop killing each other and unite and stand up, strong enough that not even a tornado can break through?

All these killings going on in the cities they label, urban.

And even higher is the number of murders that go unsolved because people refuse to speak up, not understanding there is a difference between snitching and reporting a crime, this is what the streets will not tell you.

We scream change but no change is being commanded for us killing us every day.

Voices are quiet or jumping to the defense when this conversation is brought up and no one has anything much to say.

The screams should be us uniting for a solution to preserve our youth and

Plans to stop the pain, jealousy, greed, and crime.

So many of our young souls are being gunned down in these city streets.

At an alarming rate, losing young lives to young lives between the ages of 3-18,

What is the solution because we need to save lives?

In the 2-15.

The silence in the streets must end,

Our babies deserve to live, we must stand up and show them a better way,

Because incarceration or death is not the way.

When the police kill one of us, we demand and scream for answers and justice and for the police to get what they deserve,

Our voices and demands need to be louder when one of us is behind the killing.

And not get quiet until for the family of the life lost, justice is served.

We have a Love Park, and we are supposed to be about brother and sisterhood

But filling our streets, we see more hate and blood,

We no longer live up to our name being.

The city of brotherly love.

We must do better, none of what is transpiring in our city is okay.

We must take away the violence and pain,

And put love back into the city.

And in our hearts again.

Let us together stop settling for what is wrong.

And instead, speak out and speak for what is right,

It could easily be your child being gunned down.

And you would want voices to speak up for your child, right?

But for someone you may or may not know, your thought process is, that gun violence is normal to you, so it is just another case, we will make it through,

But if all of us continue to think this way, we each fail to realize that the person hit by gunfire, could have easily been me or you.

We know the violence is out of control, and many of the youth in our families or communities are as well,

but we constantly ignore it with our silence,

There is no way we will ever be able to change our narratives.

If we refuse to do something to control or stop the violence.

I am sick and tired of waking up to the news hearing about more violence

And the number of youth lives that are dead,

And the police with the same narrative of NO MOTIVE, NO SUSPECT

With many witnesses in the communities questioned, yet no answers.

And then seeing video clips of the heartless person responsible, that left the scene and fled.

Our youth need leadership, love shown, mentoring, and to know that.

There is always a better way than being a product of their environment or needing to show off pointless skills by killing for themselves or others to prove a point.

Life as we know it and as our youth see it is becoming far too lethal,

And we are becoming desensitized as a people.

Parents: Please stop leaving your children out here alone,

Because going down the right path starts at home.

Let us build up and teach our youth to become more,

Get them eager to put down the guns and disarm the hate,

Let us show them how to bridge the gap, unite and find out their needs in an order to save them at a higher rate.

If we want to change our narratives

And preserve our youth lives, and also control and decrease the violence as a whole,

We must reach them, mind, body, and soul.

It is overdue time for us to put an end to our confusion.

I hope and pray that together we can finally come up with and effectuate a powerful solution.

TO SAVE OUR YOUTH AND STOP THE VIOLENCE…

EQUAL STANDARDS

Minds, bodies, and souls- full of

Generations of Hate, injustice, and corruption,

Personal issues since birth–that are instilled and continuously being passed on through the generations are deep-rooted.

Deep enough to destroy, like weapons of mass destruction.

You are screaming peace and equality.

But steadily bringing guns to a peaceful protest, looking for a fight

Angry if we speak up to defend ourselves or our brothers and sisters.

As if having a voice, we have no right.

We are--- judged, not by who we are, but only by our skin color,

How are we supposed to cope or survive though?

Where there is no chance given for us to even love each other?

There is no love, no respect for our lives, not an ounce of empathy,

The structure of the legal system was designed to make the unheard complexion aka us, the enemy.

We are—Tired of not breathing, tired of your foot on our necks, and feeling.

Confined,

Sick and tired of it not being justice for our lives.

And tired of seeing trying times all the time.

This is supposed to be the Land of the free,

But there is more value for a song than there is the value shown

For lives that look like me.

A system that was designed to keep us living in PO-VER-TY

While they kill us and hold us down by any means necessary.

This is the American way, the American pride,

This is their way of pushing and justifying genocide.

Claiming fear when you see us, or let us be honest, when you see our skin color.

Pretending that our men, women pose a threat to you,

When in all honesty, your hateful, racist ways shown to us, show that we are the ones that should be able to react due to fear of you.

You are all desensitized. Pulling triggers on innocent lives

Deepening our wounds as a community

As they sink deeper than the bullets that flew from your gun, followed up by the lies, coverups, and justifications,

NO! You did not fear for your life though, we fear for ours daily,

Because you are filled with hate and entitlements that have been passed.

Down through your family's generations.

Who do we call when the ones that swore to protect us are the same people?

On the other end, the killers,

While the screams get louder and more aggressive,

Screaming blue lives matter, protect the blue,

Who is going to defend us and protect us from the killer,

Who do we call when the threat on us is YOU?

Coercion, justifying, and lies getting greater while the media.

Forces the lies into minds and closed eyes,

So that it all coincides with their lies, you know.

The made-up, privileged lies.

Screaming loud "GUN"

Loud enough for it to be heard, so that it can be justified and fear to be portrayed as the reason that you chose to pull your trigger,

Yet the only thing found at the scene you had no chance to plant evidence at, is that of a hairbrush, a comb, a cellular phone,

But where is the gun that you claimed you saw? Not one in sight, GO FIGURE….

You say that we have all the same privileges. We bleed the same and we are the same,

But the truth is our lives have no value in your eyes,

Which in part makes it normal to kill our lives. If we are lucky enough

We will trend for a while and become a hash-tagged name.

We want to breathe, we want equality, not just meaningless words. We want respect for our lives. For our children's lives. We want to be free,

For the disparaging of us to stop based on the color of hate, when looking at us that you see.

 We want peace. No more promises for things to change or the lesser of what we need. We want Our lives to begin to evolve and elevate, without you all feeling that we are a threat to your existence. You say we are the same…

If that is true, stand with us and help us get to a solution,

Make for certain too that you also televise, our revolution.

We want equal standards, and WHEN YOU SEE US, SEE US!

OUR LIVES MATTER TOO

All lives matter, yes this is true.

But all we are saying, and it needs to be heard, is you cannot matter until AFRICAN AMERICAN LIVES MATTER, TOO!

I do not know if we matter or not to you,

But Our lives matter to me,

The things being done to us nowadays.

As a kid, Sorry to say, I would have never dreamed that our Men, Women, and youth would face and see.

Lives are being taken away quickly, with no remorse.

As if life, we do not deserve,

Our Demographics constantly

Being taken by those who took an oath and swore to "Protect and Serve."

TO my African American Community: Listen, we kill each other at an alarming rate.

So, to them, their thought process is why should they respect or care about us,

And more nowadays, we look at them and think, why should we in the law and system place our trust.

Our Black Men, Women, and Children, really do not even have a chance to survive,

They are killing and locking us up left and right, with no consequences, letting us know that.

We do not matter, they would rather us more dead than alive.

We are a threat to them, honestly and

We would be a greater threat if we stand up, change our narratives, and spoke up in UNITY,

As well as if we educate, support, and empower each other,

And stop degrading, hurting, and killing one another.

We as an entirety can and will only

Be able to put a stop to this and bring under control this injustice if.

In Unity, as one, we use our energy for something positive.

Breaking and disarming this cycle of hate,

Our communities must decide to take this stance together NOW.

Before it is too late!

We must stop just talking about it, we must get into action and

Be ABOUT IT,

Stop these senseless murders of other Black Kings and Queens, and the lives lost especially at the hands of this so-called LAW that is supposed to serve and protect,

Yet only there to protect and serve their own, destroy and kill us off one by one, locking us up to prevent our growth.

While justifying it all out of nothing less than for us, and our people, a lack of respect.

I am so sick of crying, being angry, and seeing or reading about

An officer killing another Black Woman, Child, or Man,

Needing no real excuses as to why except for the lie "I feared for My life."

Because the system designs it that, to kill a Black life with no consequences, they can.

ENOUGH IS ENOUGH, it is not okay!

Families lose fathers, brothers, sisters, children, wives, and husbands.

All at the hands of "The Man," and all many of us do is shake our heads,

And keep quiet until a Celebrity speaks on it, or it is our own family being shot dead.

IT IS TIME PEOPLE, speak up, they fear us more when we UNITE,

An educated, strong, powerful Black Life, especially a Black man is the worst thing to them.

He is the biggest threat, to a hate-filled man who is white.

I hate to say it that way, but it is the truth.

But it needs to be said and seen every day.

We must start getting out into our communities more and

Educating, inspiring, motivating, and preserving our youth,

Especially the youth of today.

Some police have no love for us.

Feels like we are in a guerilla warfare,

TO them our lives mean nothing to us,

So why should they care?

I am prepared and ready to create this change and what, on my part, I need to do,

My passion and my purpose are too great to give up.

It is not only about me and mine, but your lives also matter to me too.

We need no more Breonna Taylors, Xzavier Hills, Rashard Brooks, Daniel Prudes, Sean Bells, Jonathan Price's, Dijon Kizzee, Tony McDade, Sean Reeds, Atatiana Jefferson, William

Greens, Elijah McClain, Anton Blacks, Botham Jeans, Antwon Rose's, Stephon Clarks, Charlena Lyles, Deborah Danner, Tracey Williams', just to name some that many know nothing about.

We are done being silenced and families paid off after the life is taken or destroyed and justified and settled as a "wrongful death suit" or "wrongful conviction."

We will no longer accept another Black woman, youth, or man,

Being murdered, beaten, hanged, or sent to prison behind a wrongful conviction.

At the hands of an unjust system or a Policeman. WE ARE DONE! #BLACKLIVESMATTER

MISCARRIAGE OF JUSTICE

The Presumption of Innocence states "innocent until proven guilty' is a right

But that must be for those who look like the people who created it for it to go into effect,

It is a right, but not an amendment that was written in their constitution, so it was not intended

For me, to protect.

When they see us, they see a color, they never see Us for Us

Of course, they said a crime was committed, so I fit the description,

I was never treated as innocent until proven guilty,

Although they had no evidence, and no witnesses, they still handed down a sentence and wrongful conviction.

I did not do what You are accusing me of your honor,

Yet I was still questioned without my legal guardian and, coerced into a confession at an early age that destroyed my entire life, being wrongfully convicted,

Praying that the truth will someday become known

And the charges will be dropped and lifted.

Because I may or may not have been at the wrong place at the wrong time

My life has been forever changed,

For a crime, I did not commit

Standing in this courtroom in shackles and chains.

I have sisters, a mother, and I love my black women, I was a straight-A student, never been in trouble, respectful always but somehow, someway I was Lied to, accused of raping a woman that I have never even laid eyes on before

But somehow, someway, police officers pointed fingers at me, and made me the blame,

My respect for them has been changed

After this, it will never be the same.

Stripped away from my family, from my life,

Locked behind prison walls, told to get comfortable because it is my new home,

Entrapped around barbed fences, on lockdown 23 hours out of a day

No longer feeling free, being told what, when, and how I can move, my life no longer feeling like my own.

Accused from the start by police, then Wrongfully convicted, by a system that refused to believe my truth,

Lead not by reality but by their perception, filled with nothing more than generational hate, so I had to pay the cost,

At least the officer's and the court's quotas for locking away black lives have been meant

No thought of my innocence, my family, or the number of years of my life that have been lost.

While our lives chisel away and those who convict us lives tend to go on

We fight consistently trying to stay alive and afloat, while the rich get richer,

While the darkness of my situation becomes so transparent

Making it harder for me to see through the darkness, the light of justice that

They say is at the end, showing me a clearer and better picture.

I know my truth, even if they refuse to believe it or see it.

This system knows that I was dealt a corrupted and unjust hand that I did not deserve, this is true,

And with God leading, guiding, and directing my steps

The doors to this cage I am in will be opened, my voice will be amplified, for myself and others too.

It is all about holding us as the Black Family down

Keeping us separated and never able to rise above them in any shape, form, or fashion, this is my perspective, and my circumstance is my presentation,

But I refuse to allow my location or circumstance to make me give up on getting my justice

I am fully focused, dedicated, optimistic, and adamant about obtaining my exoneration.

As a youth being thrown into the eco-system of injustice, they thought they were slowing me down, stopping my elevation, and taking away my strength,

Instead, they woke me up after trying to rock me to sleep with their corruption and lies,

Being behind bars from a youth to an adult and reading every law book inside the library to help my case. Our knowledge is power, it is what they fear the most in us

They had no idea that my time spent behind bars gave me a voice, greater strength, and the knowledge I needed to set me free from what they set out to be my demise.

No, I do not want a payday which means their admittance of guilt without admitting their guilt or wrongdoing after I have lost over 20 years of my life

For me, that is not enough, exonerated now, yes, but this is not the end of my story, it is not the conclusion,

Because this System needs changing, laws rewritten and upheld

We are what we need, to completely delete the system starting with the downfall of White supremacy, and the laws written and twisted for their benefit. We need more schools for knowledge and unity of us and less racist owned institutions.

Fabulous said it best in his song "Time"

Life is too short for grudges, too long for DAs and judges, who wrongfully convict *****s

I'm talking' Central Park Five, Jena Six n****s

Exonerated, but that time still ticks n****.

Took the words right out of my mouth and my thoughts

The time handed down 20 years to life, the years went by slow,

and I lost so much throughout,

Now I am free from the walls and chains of Injustice

Innocence was taken and lost for too many years, now proven

Exonerated, and a Miscarriage of Justice.

Power of Hate

Souls being wiped away

Being preyed on from every side of the fence of violence,

Gunned down on their streets by our very own

And the citizens in the communities refused to speak up, some were forced into silence.

But do you know that when a gun is fired, the bullets always hit something

It could be your child, husband, parent, sibling, or wife,

The shooter never misses a target, even if who or what they hit was not intended.

The bullet could easily claim you, or another black man, woman, boy, or girl running for their life.

Hatred to some has a color, it is blue vs red, or white vs black.

But neither of those forms of hate shot and killed my loved one, it was the color of my skin that chose to come back and riddle his 22-year old body with bullets, striking him 4 times, with one shot being in his head,

The hate someone had for him was not about white vs black or blue vs us.

It was about the hate an individual who hated themselves yet filled with envy had toward my cousin that was so deep at that moment, he needed or wanted him dead.

Killing does not make you cool; it makes you a coward

Some bullets have no intended name. Understand that guns are not to be played with, guns are killing machines, they are not toys,

Where are the conversations and solutions to decrease the violence happening in our communities of the alarming rate of black girls and boys dying at the hands of other black girls and boys?

No one wants to have this very real conversation,

But bullets can stop more than the heart that it intended to stop,

We must stop speaking up only when the suspect is a cop.

One bullet can stop more than one heart.

Even if the bullet never touches you at all,

Because after you lose a loved one to gun violence

Your heart will never beat the same and you will never breathe the same again at all.

Losing a loved one to murder, life will never be the same.

The air you breathe is now laced with Gun powder,

All you can feel is hate for the person who took your child or loved one away.

The person that fatally gave that gun POWER.

RACISM WITH A TWIST

They no longer wear white sheets with two holes cut out in the front

Covering their heads but distinguish-Ly revealing their deceiving eyes,

They now wear in plain sight police uniforms, long black robes banging a gavel

And they wear nice suits and ties.

Still lynching us, hating us, the years changed, methods similar

But the mission is still the same,

They still lynch with guns, lies, noose, wrongful convictions, brutality, separation and degrading and holding us down, then throwing money our way

The racist's favorite and most influential game.

Racism lying and lurking within the media, aka the press

Also, within our schools, being led by none other than, the man,

With a curriculum being taught that fits their agenda enough to get us by

Keeping us ignorant and powerless is the mission. And to divide and conquer is their most effective plan.

Why don't you scream justice for us when it's our lives that are taken away?

Or when the media is disseminating misinformation and 80% of the time false lies,

Being told by the side that took life for no reason.

Instead, you stay quiet or scream; we should have complied, already assuming and making us criminals in your eyes.

That officer was full of hate and Racism

That life that was stolen never posed a threat; the officer only saw the color of their skin, he shot without a second thought, now a life no longer here,

All due to his overreaction and his cowardice fear.

They like to tell us to "get over it," and some claim racism "no longer exists.'

How can they say that when their child is safely asleep in their bed?

While ours is laying in the street for hours gunned down by that officer

That claimed he feared for his life, but our child posed him no threat, no longer alive, no respect for us or their lives, while they laugh together huddled up and our child's body lay blended in with the street for hours dead.

The normality of our lives is being taken away by Racism at the hands of those who look like you. Sentences and deaths ruled as a justification

False evidence, coercion into confessions, and made to look like the villain, but it is our fault because they should have just complied, you say

Yet, the truth of reality and facts are never taken into consideration.

We are victims of Racism every day we wake up to another day

We must fear if it will be ours or our child's last day.

Do not tell us that Racism no longer exists or

It is all within our heads because we deal with daily discrimination,

For we are victims of Racism, while you are victims of privilege

Refusing to adhere to the fact that we are not threats, we just refuse to allow any of you to make us feel any intimidation.

New year, new century, new generations, the same hate, I call it Racism with a twist

Where so many now hide behind masked blinders, seeing only fantasies, refusing to see or admit to the truth,

That even with the twist in Racism today, many are still

Using tools and tactics to defeat, confuse, keep you asleep, and destroy you.

We appreciate the ones who stand with us, rally with us, and speak out instead of being silent

Unfortunately, there are too many that get angry when we scream "Black lives matter," and they scream louder all lives matter or blue lives matter as if that will make us back down or quiet our voice,

This is not a competition of who's lives matter most. We want to exercise our rights freely and for you to realize we have never been given this option or choice.

We demand a change in policy, and the destroying of black lives and keeping us divided, and our lives treated with no value

We are demanding the courts stop justifying, and we expect accountability,

Just like if it were one of your own, being killed by one of us,

Consequences would take place without a second thought for those who inflict this fatal type of brutality.

Stop opening your mouths to continue to tell us Racism does not exist

Or that the life being gunned down or thrown behind bars for a crime they did not commit is not about race,

Never mind the facts of the reality and not the reported statistics, but it seems and proves

That we are being gunned down and locked away at much higher rates.

We go through the things we do because we are BLACK

Hmm, here is a rhetorical, but the real question for you,

Do you go through some things because you are WHITE?

Before you answer or complain about this question, please make sure you have some proof to go with your truth.

Stop saying ALL LIVES MATTER to silence our voices or make it seem that

Racism does not exist, as many of you love to shout out

Learn some facts about what we go through first, and please stop believing everything in the media or that police say happened and took place at the scene of a black life being gunned down by one of their own, put your child in the shoes of our children and yourselves in the shoes of one of us as parents, and understand our outrage, understand our anger, our fight for justice and our eyes outcried,

And further, allow your mind to be opened wide enough to realize that Racism is very much alive today. It is now called the laws of justice that protect only the privileged

It is a generational train, linked by chains, stitched together by hate and control of similar and desensitized faces and skin like yours, saying HE POSED A THREAT, OR HE HAD A GUN

Which was nothing less than made up lies, for the world to believe that we were the threat, or to yell it wasn't about race, or they should have complied, not realizing that the killing was nothing more than Racism with recorded evidence of their wrongdoing, that the courts have again justified.

NEW "N.I.G.G.A" MENTALITY

I am from the city of brotherly love, yet full of hate

With a crab in the barrel mentality, struggling to stay alive,

The families of the community are afraid to speak up and live life

Because niggas are dying daily in the trenches, fighting to survive.

I was born into poverty and- labeled a victim of the ghetto,

Forced to be a product of my environment, later labeled

A menace to society though.

No Family, All I had to turn to were the streets, welcoming me with open arms

Showing me this false kind of love and protection from all the pain,

With me realizing when it is too late that

My real family and my street family's intentions were all the same.

I took one for the team to prove my loyalty to those pretending to have my back though,

Up here alone receiving no visitors, Snitching is not an option,

Staying silent, and taking the rap saves my life though.

I was born with this n.i.g.g.a mentality yet labeled a menace to society.

I was raised by the streets, but book smart too, but I had to survive

Hustlin' with the best strategy,

I witnessed so much growing up

So much pain, loss, trauma, and tragedies.

Grew up in a home full of no love, only neglect,

Ran with the streets of this city

Running into nothing more than betrayal, disloyalty, and disrespect.

Growing up a black man in the hood

In their eyes, we are supposed to be dead or in jail some say

They label most of us as just another nigga, a waste of life, and,

Never to grow up to be as intelligent, successful, or important

As the white man.

You see where I come from, we are

Destined to fail and kill each other,

Taught to show no love, only hate, for one another.

The struggle is real out here

I am just a black man trying to make a living,

No jobs, no tangible way of life besides the street corners

Which for all of us was a given.

Everything about us is looked at as wrong,

We are labeled ghetto, loud, ignorant, jealous of, and taught to hate one another,

Yet we are products of the environments created for us back when

To keep us down and turning against each other.

Born with this n.i.g.g.a mentality yet labeled a menace to society.

I was Born with this n.i.g.g.a mentality yet labeled a menace to society.

Listen: Their definition of a "nigga"

Is nothing more than something disrespectful, something that

means we will never amount to anything more because we

struggle and live-in poverty with no silver spoon,

But this city taught us survival, but we are also learning that

Our power will shine through soon.

No worries, we will be "niggas" meaning

Never Ignorant Getting Goals Accomplished

As soon as we decide to unite, wake up, and realize,

That we are fighting and killing one another, and helping them

rid and keep us grounded

While they sit back laughing and finding new ways to divide

and conquer, pulling the wool over our eyes.

They label us a menace to society, but no we are

A City learning the new "N.I.G.G.A" mentality.

THEY PREY

It is so much corruption in the system.

Time is over-due for us to open our eyes up,

They are preying on, harassing, and killing our babies.

Because they are taught and trained to stop us from rising up.

You see, us standing together and supporting each other and

Understanding that our power is knowledge and unity

this we all must realize,

Because while we continuously hate and kill each other, they are consistently

Killing our youth, sweeping it under the rug, and telling more lies.

The justice system as a whole is responsible for the lives, the police

Gun down and the courts excuse every time,

With no punishment, just paid leave, temporary desk duty for these suspects.

For their justifiable hate crimes.

The "He got a gun" lie they love every time to shout,

So, it is heard over the police radio, yet never in police view or the dashcam or body camera.

So that it makes it easier for the self-defense plea and the rest of the lies to come out.

Ignoring the cries of our babies screaming "I can't breathe" or "my hands are up."

Yet they still shoot, punch, or choke them, while witnesses scream "stop please don't,

This nonsense must stop, but we all know that it won't.

Black lives have no chance at life.

No chance to survive,

They must guard themselves against every angle.

And fight regardless to stay alive.

Our babies cannot even go outside to play, buy candy, wear hoodies, sell CDs,

Fix their cars, exercise, enjoy the night before their wedding, or walk down the street,

Without being harassed by police or their affiliates and wondering if death is waiting for them to meet.

They scream protect and back the blue, while they gun down our Queens and have their knees in the necks of our Kings, talking about they should've "complied."

Yet refusing to release the dashcam footage, so now how about.

The police should not have lied.

Afraid of our knowledge and unity which is our greatest power.

But they continue to lie claiming the gun allegation,

For their reasons to kill them

With cases of no charges and ends with a justification.

You see, our melanin and beauty are why they are jealous of us, which poses a threat.

Making them want to pull a gun,

Therefore, I am the voice that will not be silenced and will fight to save and preserve our babies, I will not stop or give up, no matter how hard it will get, because we all matter and I am the voice for the voiceless, dead, or alive and

I know that with patience and dedication, the changes that I am speaking up about and working for will come!

WE REPRESENT STRENGTH

What should we tell our black brothers, sons, husbands, cousins, nephews, or friend?

When they are stopped by or see a police officer coming their way,

Should we tell them to comply

Or should we tell them to turn and run away?

You see, our instincts tell us to advise them to listen

And to do exactly what they say and never look as if they are reaching,

However even that is not helping them to stay alive, and the system shows that whatever an officer does it is okay,

At least that is what they are teaching.

Law showing that it is okay for them to shoot our unarmed black men

And the courts let them off, saying the shootings are justified,

So, they continue to destroy the lives of our black boys, girls, and men

Be it guns, beating, assassination, mass incarcerations, or just like back in the day lynching or being crucified.

YES! I said lynching,

So many of our black youth are being found hanged. In 2018 they lynched a young black man name Danye Jones in Missouri

Still trying to convince the public that they are committing suicide,

But the way he hung with a noose around his neck, face bruised, pants to his ankle, arms at his side with his fist clenched closed

There is no way he killed himself, this was a definite message sent, this was a homicide.

They are preying on our black lives daily

Looking to rid the world of us, in the best way that they can,

Focusing on keeping us divided or keeping us down,

That is why I do not get why we are killing and destroying one another, and I do not understand.

We have a greater enemy that we cannot fight alone

We cannot be the voices of our communities and preach unity

If we continue to show for one another, a lack of respect,

We must come together in unity and show them

That we will no longer tolerate this nonsense

And the murder of our black lives, we will no longer accept.

How many more of our loved ones must die or be sentenced to lose their life for life, behind a petty crime not fitting the sentence?

We are now living in the days we read about in school, nothing has changed,

The faces preying on us are all the same, with different names

Yet the hate for black lives remains.

All we have is just us, we are our justice

Because the laws are designed only for them

Victims are unarmed, with no records, yet lives are being taken away

Justified by their laws, self-defense being claimed,

Covered up for months, protecting the suspects

And the victim and families are being blamed.

We are not going to be moved or silenced

Nor allow them to make us fear them.

We want answers, we demand peace,

We demand something be done

To these murderous police.

Hands UP! Don't shoot, don't lynch, don't abduct, don't threaten our lives for speaking out

They scream justice for all, but honestly, they show that for black lives, freedom is not free,

Our families seem to become more of a target when we speak out and fight

For our equality.

We have read about these days while in school, learning their curriculum

In our class of social studies, or as they called it, our "history,"

Claiming times have changed,

Yet I see not much of a change, let alone a victory.

We demand a change; it is time for us to act

I have black brothers, a black nephew, a black cousin, a black child

And I care about all black lives, our skin is all the same,

We may look a bit different, but we all deal with the effects

Nationwide Of this undying pain.

I stand in support of black lives beginning to matter to us

So that we can demand that they matter to others

We will no longer allow or accept these officers or courts to use us as target practice

Leaving our streets in the community painted red,

Locking up our innocent black lives or handing down sentences that do not match the crimes

Nor will we allow them to continue to justify or cover up the shit that they did.

It is becoming harder and harder for me to see our black lives in anything besides a coffin

Or locked away in a penitentiary, being mixed up in the system

With a false or wrongful conviction,

Most often due to the case of how they say it,

"Fitting the description."

We stand up and speak out so that we can have no more:

Brandon Tate Brown, Philando Castile, Eric Garners, Sandra Bland, Rakia Boyd, Tamir Rice, Trayvon Martins, Antwan Rose, Danye Jones, Kendrick Johnson, Emmitt Till, Trayvion

Blount, Central Park 5's, Terrence Crutcher, Oscar Grant Jr's, Stephon Clarks, Sam Dubois, Freddie Greys, Akia Gurley, and Kalief Browder.

Our revolution is just getting started,

Until we see a change within this unjust ass system, they call the LAW

Our movements are here to stay,

And through our platforms, our voices will be heard and respected

Our messages are loud and clear, and they will pay attention to the words that we have to say.

NO LONGER A NIGHTMARE

She was a beautiful woman, with an unforgettable smile, kindhearted, who loved the wrong one for too long.

A mother, a grandmother, an aunt, a cousin, a daughter, a friend,

Who would make up herself sometimes for the world to see,

But only to hide the person she needed to hide because she could no longer be who she wanted to be.

She would wear her hair on her face sometimes and wear more make-up than usual, and clothes that were able to hide certain aspects of her.

But you see, behind her make-up hid secrets she kept in the dark,

Underneath her clothes and fake smile carried pain

Underneath the makeup on her face carried years of abusive marks.

He pretended well, or so he thought he did.

It all began a little after they met,

She said she forgave him though after

The first time he uttered a threat.

He apologized and placed the blame on a bad day at work or her,

After every time he landed a punch on her beautiful face,

And often she blamed herself for saying that.

She must have forgotten her place.

Every time after the hits, he would Soon hit her with the "I'm sorry. "

And it will never happen again speech,

But it still felt like in those moments that.

For her, he had a lesson to teach.

To make her fear him or put her in check,

to correct her ways,

The abuse, cheating, manipulation, and womanizing became a normal thing,

But her love for him was strong for a while, she could not just give up on him at first, but then it became too much, and her life began to go by in a daze.

She finally started to be happy again and could breathe and had finally freed herself of this man she once loved, although still afraid of him still

But He had moved away, she could now live and smile again.

As she began getting her voice back and feeling herself again and living life.

He showed up on New Year's Eve unannounced and took her life.

If she could speak, this is what I believe she would say:

For you see, I am no longer, I am a dream.

All because no one ever took notice of my changes or silent screams.

The police never made me a priority.

They never protected me.

He hit me so hard that I didn't come around.

And he just left me there, in a heap of blood in my bathroom on the ground.

The neighbors heard all the cries and commotion.

People saw him and he was described as 'devoid of emotion.'

You see he killed me that day because I wanted to leave the marriage, I needed to breathe, needed some peace and my air,

My friends, children, and his son's mother had always told me to beware.

But you see, now it's too late, for so long he had me too scared.

And now I have been Killed by the one whose life I shared.

He claimed to others that someone else did it to me that he was friends with or that I had fallen, and he was out of town, he wasn't home.

But somehow, they found him to be lying, they found him a month later in another state, hiding out with a woman, who believed he was innocent and says he was with her, not in Virginia at my home.

He has hurt others and his child, his record proves that, And the system and his family failed him long ago.

And now I am gone a lifetime away from my children because he refused to just let me go

The system failed me even more.

But now he is locked up for LIFE I hope, so he cannot hurt anyone anymore.

But for me, now it is too late, I am sure some ask, "why didn't she just leave"? Let them know I tried, which is why I am no longer here in the flesh only in a dream because I tried to leave him,

But my only hope is that my story will help someone's life or a family member's life be less painful and less grim.

VOICELESS VOICES: Words from a Broken Heart & Renewed Soul

In memory of Sammy L Barnes

Voiceless Solitude

The secrets and verbal abuse I kept to myself.

So that no one would know,

The black eyes, the bruises on my neck covered with make-up.

Pretending we were happy, so in love around family and friends, we would put on a show.

I loved you with every bone and breath in my body.

But the love was never really reciprocated, you only wanted to control me,

You apologize over and over, and I believe you and that it would get better.

That you would never intentionally set out to destroy or hurt any part of me.

I cover up tears and hope that nothing I do will bring out your anger.

And make you strike me out in public for all to see,

That the highs of your love and control over my life

were beginning to slowly blind me.

My family never knew that I was suffering abuse.

At the hands of the man who called me his wife,

The one I would give up everything for

The one I vowed to love for the rest of my life.

The man that I have been through hell and back with

Since I was a teenager, but only loved you still.

Even when you were away, my heart was only yours

Yet I am the one you hurt consistently, and I am afraid that you may someday kill.

I have never been afraid to fight back no matter who came at me.

Never been afraid to let my voice or opinions be heard,

But for some reason or another, I cannot bring the strength to fight you

Or even speak a word.

For a while, you would never leave bruises that people could see

You would never hit me in my face,

So that when I would go out, there would be no questions.

And your persona could be kept undercover, and you would never feel out of place.

I remember you came into the house one night, quiet, as I was on the phone with one of my best friends.

As I turned around you punched me in my face and I do not even know the reason why,

All I know is that night with each hit.

I was sure that at that moment that I was going to die.

My son was in the other room as you constantly beat on me, I could not think through the panic.

I could not fight back through the fear,

Your endeavors to harm me for your reasons.

Were all too clear.

To die at the hands of the one my children call their father.

The one who said that he loved me, who asked me to marry him and become his wife,

The one I go to bat for even against my own family.

The one who promised to love and protect me forever is now the one I need protecting from

You are the one I now fight at this moment to breathe, no strength to fight, no courage to speak, to save my own life.

You told me that you would kill me downstairs in our living room.

Drag me upstairs and put me into a tub of water in the bathroom and,

Ransack the house, kidnap my son, and make it look like a robbery gone bad.

Do you call this love? I call this possession, control, and behavior like one I will never understand.

I feared this man, I loved this man, I believed he would change. He broke me down.

He convinced me no one else would want me, I believed If I left that I would gain nothing but that I would lose,

So, I stayed and continued to suffer before he left visual scars.

In the plight of my life to be broken, battered, raped, and abused.

Eve said that "Love is Blind,"

But honestly, is it? Am I stupid for staying after the first time, some say yes, and some say no?

I say you must be in it to understand or realize that it's more than stupidity.

It is control over the mind for someone else's enjoyment and strength. It is the fear of threats often of what will happen if you do decide to go.

Do not judge me. Do not judge her. Do not judge him. For staying. Or as you say, "putting up with it" It is not that easy all the time to just get up and leave.

My son saved my life on that night he set out to kill me.

God stepped in right in time through my son, God saved me, but not everyone could be saved from their abusers. So, for the ones that are still here and who may endure this someday, I stand with you, I speak for you. We are the voices for the voiceless, and if they were here, they would say loud and clear NO MORE:

No more walking on eggshells

No more sitting on the edge of my seat.

No more huddled in the corner apprehensively

No more sobbing my heart out.

No more putting on a brave face.

No more fearing what mood you are in.

No more hiding my scars with make-up.

No more lying to my loved ones.

No more fear of being judged.

No more crying out for help in frightened whispers.

No more of your family or friends turning a blind eye or blaming me.

No more watching what I have to say.

No more teasing me with your fists

No more of your plausible lies

No more presuming the Law would come to my rescue or make me a priority.

No more threats

No more being at the receiving end of your substance abuse or your fist.

No more feeling nauseous deep within my soul.

No more of me coming last on your list of priorities.

No more trusting you.

No more excuses

No more cruel mind games

No more exploitation of my painful past and using it against me.

No more making me feel insecure or not worthy.

No more playing on my vulnerabilities.

No more accusations

No more hiding behind false smiles

No more of your intimidation

No more being stabbed in the back by you and my so-called friends.

No more bullying me to get what you want.

No more broken promises to change.

No more being taken advantage of

No more forgiveness

No more fighting for 'our' family

No more pleas

No more of my children staring at their tear-stained Mother.

No more manipulation of all those around us

No more unwarranted aggression

No more yielding to your fake ass tears

No more fear

No more Nightmares

No more Heartache.

No more staring the enemy in the face....

Listen: Please Gain awareness of the severity of abuse

Stop judging because it is not easy as many may think to just walk away.

Too many lives have been lost at the hands of Domestic Abuse and Violence

Sometimes the signs are there, sometimes they are not because they are hidden for fear of judgment.

How many people do you know that suffer from domestic abuse or lost life behind it? Of three of your friends, it could be one or be two,

As numbers compare, one day, it could even be you.

PROUD TO BE ME (GAY PRIDE)

My first love hurt me deeply

He took and broke so many pieces of my heart,

He left me with unanswered questions back then

And a tainted heart he just ripped apart.

As I have gotten older, I can now say

Now I understand why he turned his back, he ran away,

Why there was no way

That I could make him stay.

He was afraid to love me, afraid peers would judge him

Afraid to stay and take a chance,

Afraid to admit to himself or others who he is

Afraid to stand up or take a stance.

He would have rather taken a chance to stay in the closet

Or inside of his mind, which was like a jail,

He would rather stay pretending for society

Although on my end, for him, I sacrificed and paid the bail.

I came out of the closet, told my parents

They said it is just a phase, that I will get over it soon,

While others speak hateful words to me and try to hurt me, hoping to kill us in the end,

But none of that will make us be who they think we should be

None of these actions will make us give in.

What is the other's point of judging or trying to hurt us, to make us feel less than or bad?

So, we can understand the world

What it is like to be lonely and sad?

We do not need your intentional hate for us

Because we already know how it feels,

To be hated, judged, spoken ill on with family disowning us,

We know already which is why we keep who we are a secret so much, it is a sense of self, we cannot seem to reveal.

Why does it affect you, what I like and who I like to be with?

If you are secure in your manhood, why does it matter what we do,

Why do you hate me, or do I make you feel disgusted?

How exactly is my lifestyle choice affecting you?

I do not judge you for how you live your life

Or the mistakes that any of you choose in the least bit,

Because what you eat or drink

Don't make me shit.

It is not about us as individuals that so many of you hate

It is more about the love that you have for yourself,

We love exactly who we are

We are tired of being who the world thinks we should be, and

Continuing to lie and hide who we are in ourselves.

I like who I like, I love who I love,

I am Gay and I am proud to be ME,

I am sorry if my lifestyle disgusts you,

But it is who I choose to be.

Later, in life, even my parents will see

That the reason I am gay is that I am being ME.

Today, I take a stand

And let the world know that, YES, I am gay,

And guess what else,

I would not have it any other way.

UNHEALED

All I ever wanted was love from you, mom

But all my life you turned your back on me,

You chose your husband's side over mine too many times before

Which put a burning flame of rage inside of me.

The hate that I feel in me for him

For all the disgusting things that he put me through,

I cannot even begin to explain

Let alone explain the feelings inside of me that I feel today toward you.

I was consistently getting beaten,

Verbally abused and never treated well,

I was the young teenage boy

Whose life was a living hell

Thrashes on my back, whelps on my ass from his belt,

And from his fist, bruises on my face,

I could not defend myself, all I could do is ball up in a corner

Praying for God to remove me from that place.

I wanted to die so many times while enduring the abuse

I felt no love 80% of the time, in what was supposed to be a HOME,

Yes, you made sure I had the necessities needed in my life,

With a house full of people, I still felt alone.

No woman should ever allow any man to abuse her children

Or show them a lack of respect,

And no woman should call herself a mother if her children

She refuses to love equally or to protect.

Numerous nights you let him send me to bed without eating

What type of human being would do this to another person,

especially a child he was supposed to play a father figure to,

The sad reality for me is that I felt more love and protection behind the walls

Then in over 20 years, mom that I have felt from you.

You feel no remorse even after your husband is a lifetime away, no apology, just expect me to go on in life building a relationship with you moving forward pretending to be there for me now, but what about WHEN,

And it hurts because even today, I would give my life for you,

If you love me, mom, all I want is to be shown and you to stop making me feel like I am the mistake in the end.

You, laid down and made me, you had me, yet you said nothing at all

you chose that man over me my entire life and expect me now to just forget all the abuse and the lies,

All the scars he left throughout my body

And all the tears that left my eyes.

You said nothing to protect me, your child, your son,

I was not the perfect child or teenager, and I am not the perfect adult

All I wanted was a mother like everyone else, but I did not seem to have one.

But if I can be honest, I cannot even love myself or anyone else because of my motherly issues

and all the trauma that I was made to endure,

You may not want to hear what I have to say, but my truth is my truth

And my pain is not something anyone can take from me or make me hide anymore.

Like a fire burning through a tree

The pain from all these years of this concealed pain has taken over and controlled me.

All I ever wanted from you was to know that I mattered to you

And for once, you to choose me over him, your husband, your man,

And for you to stop the abuse from taking place

Now, all I want is for you to acknowledge your wrongdoing and stop pretending it did not happen, stop being in denial, and open yourself enough to listen to me, your son, and to understand.

Looking all depressed is what I do best,

But trying to survive is a big test.

I am a grown man, still filled with hurt, resentment, and rage

Pushing people away from me who genuinely love me or want to help me, even at this age.

But because of unhealed and unresolved parts of me, I do not even know how to love myself.

Let alone, to open me up to let anyone in or love anyone else.

Today, I choose to learn to love me and to forgive you and him

I choose to stop allowing my past to control me,

I release the pain that destroyed my entire life today,

Even if I never hear the words that I have been wanting to hear you say.

Forgiving is for me, my sanity matters, and I deserve to live, to be free

I deserve to be loved, every, single part of me.

INNOCENCE LOST

You control my mind to the extent that you choose.

You have me right where you want me to be, doing as you want me to.

Mentally breaking me down, making me believe

No one will ever love me as much as you do.

Mind totally on you, and only you and doing as you want.

Terrified to speak up, or allow my voice to be heard,

Falling deeper and deeper into this love I think is real.

Mentally enslaved and afraid to ever speak a word.

I am all the way in and, it is hard to get out.

Your primary goal is to feel strength from this mind manipulation,

What is hurting me, and many others, is giving you this crazy

Type of strengthening from this victimization.

You have taken a community of young women.

And created a cult to fulfill your stimulation,

Putting women into your controlling graces and an uncomfortable form of isolation.

Hmm. You seemed so great at first, you were like a mentor.

Someone that I saw as family and with whom I felt protected,

The one who I looked up to and I thought loved me like family.

The one who I always respected.

Only to finally realize the love and respect that you showed.

Was about more than that, you were a predator,

Hurting young women like me,

Pulling them in close enough to do what you wanted.

And to be only what you allowed them to be.

The control, the mind control that you had gave you strength.

It gave you power, this is what I believe to be true,

The same amount of power that you take from young women.

Was a power taken away at an early age from you?

It does not make it right though, no matter what anyone says.

You took the trust from those of us who cared for and looked up to you, and gave us not an ounce of respect,

You seduced us with your gifts, your confidence, and everything about you was so different.

Then the person that when looking at you, that I would expect.

Yes, everyone has fantasies in life, but

What is it that you could see or be attracted to by sexing and controlling a younger girl,

Coming into our lives pretending to be one thing, and turning out to be

Someone whose only priority is destroying our worlds.

Keeping my story to myself, afraid to speak out.

Bottled up with days and days of silent tears,

Never being able to tell my story to others.

For way too many years.

Afraid that no one would ever believe me.

Because of the weight and popularity that you carry and who you are to so many

Later to find out that you not only did this to me,

But you did this to far too many.

Thankful to finally be able to talk to someone.

Although those around you, knew of all the victims and things you did, and they chose to be quiet about,

I am glad that I am finally able to open up and share my story.

And let this pain out.

All this time has gone on and I felt weak.

I just could not go forward with my life for far too long,

But thanks to the #metoo movement, we as women can now take back our power.

And be strong, for we too are strong.

I will no longer allow this person to have this control over me.

Or continue to hold me captive by staying quiet, I choose to step over the line,

To finally tell my truth and let out this secret, of the years that I was physically, sexually, and mentally abused and controlled in my mind.

None of this was or is okay, it has destroyed all my relationships, until now

But I feel better knowing that I am not alone.

But sorry to hear that there were plenty others,

But happy that our stories are being shared,

 not only gave us back our strength.

But we will be able to save another.

THE PAINS I HIDE

I lost my peace, my smile, my heart

I lost myself as an entirety. I felt numb and void inside.

No one to turn to or vent to, no one to call on

No one to confide in with all the pain that I hide.

How am I supposed to feel after witnessing the murder of someone I am close to?

This murder I speak of that destroyed my being has a plot twist,

I am a witness to a cold-hearted murder. The victims are me and my innocence

He destroyed my life. And it all began at age six.

The crime scene was abnormal, inside of my bedroom, inside of our home

Forced into silence around family and made to hide the tears in my eyes,

But he had mama controlled and hypnotized to a point that she would not have believed me, her daughter anyway

She would have believed all his lies.

The pain I held inside, the sadness on my face, the shivers when he came around. A mother should have known, she should have seen.

But she did not care enough to find out or want bad enough to know,

Most will never understand

Because most of my scars I just could not show.

A Confirmed forced entry from a rape kit at my doctor's office, would have been my only evidence

He was careful never to leave a clue or a single trace,

Except for the memories hidden deep inside of me,

Which even now, I can never erase.

I can still feel him touching me, grabbing me, and forcing my body closer to his

It still feels so real, even when he appears inside of my dreams,

Pressing his penis inside of me over and over, with a smile on his face

Covering my mouth with his hands, so that I do not scream,

The last time he took it, I tried to fight back in hopes to loosen his grip

But he would not let me go, he pressed me harder into the bed,

He made me relive my fears, but also made me wish even more that I was dead.

Because of him, I cannot trust anyone, I hate the world, especially men

The me that you once knew is dead, and I feel empty inside too,

I have hurt myself throughout the years trying to erase the rest of me because He murdered me long ago.

Like some murders, the police never found my body

Because, unlike the usual murder, my body is still around,

I am a real live prisoner stuck inside of my skin

An adult woman walking around wounded, scarred, lost, and constantly wondering if I will ever be found.

The girl my family once knew is no longer here

She was lost at the age of six and life chiseled away every time he touched me, this pain I still hide, the differences in me and the isolation issues, why does not anyone care enough to notice and see,

That the girl Inside of my body was lost long ago

She is no longer inside of me.

There was never a service for my murder

Because no one knew that I had died,

But this is what happens when

A pain this deep, we hide deep inside.

THE LESSON

It controls her, she can't' seem to stop it

It is a constant battle, but the razor, she cannot seem to drop it.

Thoughts of no one loving her started it all, it turned into a habit that she cannot quit,

Taking over her mind and her body, little by little, bit by bit.

Each time, the scar fade away, they disappear after a while

But unlike the faded scars, the heartbreak and the memories from the pain do not,

No matter how bad she desires for the pain to be forgotten, they will not.

It is a constant struggle, a war that never seems to end,

It is an ongoing battle that she never seems to win.

Picking up a razor when the tears start to fall again

Or the hurt again invades her space,

She believes she has control over her pain with the cutting, it is her sweet escape

With every cut, her adrenaline begins to race.

One day I hope that she will listen to me because I care

And leave that razor in the cabinet and not pick it up in her hand,

But as of now, it is a pain she is unable to withstand.

As the world around her seems to move on for some

But for others, it just seems to stand still,

People judge her for what she does because no one cares enough to understand

If you have not gone through what she had, you never will.

He hurt her again with his words, his rejection, his cheating ways, and he hangs up

The Tears have her dizzy once again, as she presses the razor deeper into her cheek

And her head getting light,

This time she is tired of stopping, tired of trying, she has had enough

She falls back on the bed after she turns out the light

As she takes one last breath and closes her eyes. Thinking it is again just for the night.

This time she cut too deep because the call that I Got said she is gone.

Laying down to sleep last night was not temporary, she is gone for good,

She thought she was just going to sleep not dying, but in honesty

We both knew that someday she would.

She felt alone every day like she had no one to turn to but tears and a razor, although it was the result of why she was hurting,

But the cutting and the scars felt better than the way he treated her as if, for him and her parents, she was a burden.

She came to me in my dreams to tell me that she apologizes for being so weak

She said that she is not sure why he was able to break her so deep

And she wished that she had just stopped as I asked numerous times and allowed me to help her get better. She is not sure what she allowed herself to become,

She wishes that she could turn back the hands and make a different choice

But it is too late for her now because the lights of death and life have already come.

She wants everyone to tell themselves who are going through the habit of cutting

That you will get through the pain that pushed you to this point, instead choose LIFE,

Instead of picking up a razor, a gun, or a knife.

Your life matters, you can recover,

You will get through all of this, just take it day by day, believing and not giving up.

In the words of Motivational Speaker and Hip-Hop Preacher Eric "ET" Thomas

You Can, You Will, You Must!

THEY DESTROYED ME

We should never judge a book by its cover, some say.

Because we never have any idea of what someone may have gone through,

While trying to destroy them or their character

We end up destroying ours in the long run too.

Some folks in life seem to say and do things as they feel.

And through popularity and fear, it seems to be what is allowed.

And it happens more than often nowadays in schools, at work, or on social media.

To fit in with what they deem as the "it", or popular crowd.

Students and so-called friends spreading rumors about the next

People follow suit because they think it is what they should do, it is what popularity is about,

Not caring how much they are hurting someone else or destroying their mental

And the person being destroyed, feeling that there is no way out.

Sitting off to themselves while at school, at work, or out in the community, or quiet to themselves when at home,

Afraid to speak a word of it to their parents, so in a journal they write,

And oftentimes the journal entries are about ending it all.

Rather it is their own or someone else's life.

When? When will we as people learn to understand and see the signs?

That shows something is going on with our loved ones because oftentimes they are there,

But it takes patience and the willingness to learn and to bring awareness.

So that we can save a life, while they are still here.

Bringing awareness to, and spreading the word of the severity of bullying and depression is needed now,

By reaching out in unity, we can save so many lives, and bridge the gap before too long,

There is no more time for us to decide to wait until the last minute to take the blindfolds off

The change starts with us with which we are among.

Too many lives are being destroyed one by one, kid by kid, family by family.

Hiding their depression and anger, dealing with it in their hand,

Not knowing how to ask for help or speak out.

Dealing with what they are made to endure, in the best way that they can.

If it is being bullied in school, at home, out in their community, or cyberbullied, either way, it needs to stop.

The old saying, "words will never break me" are a lie because words do hurt.

They tear right on through and destroy day by day,

Breaking down an individual more

With pieces of them constantly chiseling away.

Waiting to get away to be alone and able to cry.

So, no one can gossip more and make fun of them, so they hide their tears,

And no one notices the signs of the change in the person, or maybe they do.

But they decide to stay quiet, either due to the need to fit in

Or retaliation fears.

We do not realize how serious bullying or depression is.

So many make fun of it

Often due to lack of caring or failure to understand,

Then you have others who think their cries for help are for the attention

So, they ignore it, instead of doing all that they can.

There is nothing else that they can do.

The pain of these individuals they can no longer take,

Sick and tired of having to come face to face with what has already destroyed their life.

There is nothing else for them to take.

Thoughts of getting a weapon and going to school or work to take away all the lives.

That set out daily to destroy her or him,

As well as all the teachers and employees, or counselors that chose to not care enough to see an issue.

They want also to destroy all of them.

They just want It all to stop, and to feel happy and free.

There is no one to turn to, no one that they trust enough to confide,

So instead of the continuous pain and tears

They decide to commit SUICIDE!

Hell of a Master

I have a new master, one different than the one that you know

My master is one of the evilest types and kind,

He controls every part of my body, making me feel wanted, no longer alone

He took over every part of my being, including my health and my mind.

He searches for his next victim and figures out when is the perfect time to engage,

Doesn't discriminate on gender, race, size, or age.

This master of mine has different aliases, he goes by

Crystal, Yayo, Nose Candy, Crack, Tussin, White Girl, Uppers, Black Beauties, Bath Salts, Xanax, Alcohol Addiction, Molly, or Ice,

Just to name a few aliases of my new master that has me under his control

If you encounter him, go the opposite way,

please I beg you to learn from my story and take my advice.

This is my life, my story, my pain, it has not been easy, it is not a game,

No person should ever have to be forced into life from this Master, of misery or shame.

He will make you believe that what is hurting you,

The drugs will make it disappear,

Make you feel like what he has for you, will make you feel free, no longer living in fear.

When he introduced himself to me, he introduced himself as

As my very own new way of coping with my pain of life,

My self-conviction,

It has destroyed my life in every way, I lost everything and everyone

He lied to me, the fix was only temporary,

but I needed it more, it became a real live addiction.

He is a master of manipulation

Making you fall right into his lap

Fighting to get away, after being pulled completely into his trap.

Your heart turns cold as you play the game.

Your life as of now will never be the same.

Do not pass go – strip your dignity right here.

No one else loves you like me, He will say, so dry your tears,

Your Self-respect is long forgotten,

You would sell your soul to the devil for an Oxycontin.

Your Addiction, Life, and your faithful Friend.

He will tell you that he has your back from now on and will stick it out 'til the end.

For the master, those drugs, you traded your dreams, goals, and those who love you, for that destination that was stuck in your head!

One hell of a master wasn't he, Welcome to the train of Hell,

Next stop... Well, there is none, it is too late because now she is dead.

Please if know someone battling addiction of any kind, you do not have to go through it alone, there is a better way, or if you are battling addiction, contact someone close to you OR call 1-800-662-4357. Talk to someone Today.

LIFE FOREVER CHANGED

(Loss of a Child to Murder)

My life has changed in the worst way forever

I would not wish anyone to ever feel this way,

The only words I can speak now it seems are Justice or Why

Because I have no idea other than that what to say.

My days are filled with tears, barely any smiles

And countless times throughout the day I just want to scream,

Steady Hoping that you come walking through the door

Telling me this has been nothing more than a bad dream.

The aches and pains deep inside of my heart

It will never go away,

my breath and my life were removed and stolen

on the night, those cowards took you away.

Our worlds have been turned upside down

It has been changed from black to gray,

How do we go on without you?

This is a question I ask every day.

I do not know who I am anymore

I no longer feel like me,

Most people see a grieving parent who lost their child, and it is all they see when they look at Me.

So many people are silent, refusing to speak up and give us the answers needed to give you justice,

While others choose not to care because it did not affect their own,

But what they fail to understand is,

A child is left without a mother or father, siblings left without, a parent without a child and it destroyed my home.

I lay my soul down to sleep every night as I pray

And with every time I hear your name,

They say time heals all pain, but as of right now

Time proves my soul will never be the same,

I am missing you dearly my child

I cannot get any rest tonight, I cannot close my eyes to sleep,

Time is not healing this wound

The pain is too deep.

I will not stop fighting until justice is served

And someone steps up giving you your voice back and mines too,

Until that day, even with the tears, we will continue to

Focus on getting justice for you.

A life cut short, a scream in the night, blindsided by those you trusted

The wound, the pain, the hurt is one like no other,

These are feelings of a grieving father or mother.

VOICELESS VOICES: Words from a Broken Heart & Renewed Soul

SECTION II: EXHAUSTED BLACK WOMAN

"While one may encounter many defeats, one must not be defeated"

Maya Angelou

BROKEN

We must learn to let go.

And get up from the table when love is no longer being served,

Especially if the one that we love so much.

Is treating us worse than what we deserve.

You cannot go on hurting yourself.

By trying to hold on, you must let go,

Because if they loved you in return

They would not allow any disrespect to show.

They would put you above everyone else.

They would place you first without a doubt,

Then rather than proving they do not want you.

They would prove to you; that you, they do not want to live without.

Do not keep allowing yourself the pain.

And tears, or the broken pieces of your heart,

Stop making them a priority when you are.

Only a piece of the option, an exceedingly small part.

Being on the side, woman or man, makes you look stupid.

There Is no way or room in their heart for you to win,

You must cut all ties now.

And never allow yourself this type of predicament ever again.

You tend to lose yourself completely in it.

You lose your self-esteem, self-confidence, character, worth, and all that you forget,

With all that loss, your tears and hurt build up more.

And getting all of it back will be hard to get.

Why would a person be out to use and hate you this much?

Someone you cared for, yet all they give you is constant rejection,

Along with all the lies, deceit

And stolen affections?

He never belonged to only you.

His love was all along with someone else,

Honestly ask yourself this question: How can you believe his words when.

He cannot even be loyal and true to himself?

Never trust a man who is pursuing women.

Who he knows he cannot be loyal to,

Because he will set out to only

hurt and use you.

So, wipe your eyes my sister, and mend your heart.

And realize not everyone is loyal, please listen to and believe me,

You must find a way to let go and move on

And just let that man be.

CAN YOU SEE ME?

I am so tired. Tired of hiding my pain or hiding who I am underneath this mask.

Pretending that everything is fine, everything is alright.

Pretending to be happy and full of life

When everything is tearing into me, day by day, little by little.

Having to be strong to the point that I am slowly breaking because

I do not know how to let this go, and to go on within my life, to the point that I can enjoy LIFE. I do not know who I am, but my question is, CAN YOU SEE ME?

You say that you do not understand my feelings or what depression feels like.

You ask me what it feels like. Well, to be honest, Depression is feeling like I just cannot be happy long enough without anger or tears flowing down my face.

It feels like I am clicking up a roller coaster slow in slow motion

Waiting for it to reach its peak, yet never seeming to reach the top.

Many people call me heartless. They feel as though my mouth is ruthless. That I say what I want. That I have no feelings because "I am just like a man." But the truth is, I do have feelings to an extent, but my insides are destroyed, and I hide them the best way that I can by trying to be there for others and motivate them to be better. I hide the things that I have gone through to an extent, in an order to take attention from my own life and focus on helping others to understand themselves or their behaviors. I wonder if people even realize

How difficult it is for me somedays to function,

Especially for someone who is not sure if they even exist. CAN YOU SEE ME?

Depression has been described to me as having a disinterested corpse

Stowed inside the shell of a body whose insides are gone.

I used to laugh all the time

I cannot even begin to explain to you what exactly, now is missing, because I do not know,

I wear this mask daily so you cannot see me

and my pain and hurt will not show.

When I am alone, and by myself, my tears can flow without pity or judgment

I can remove this mask from my face, and my soul can be broken free out of this hidden shell,

I can allow the unhappiness and the tears to break free

And unleash the anger within me from hell.

But for now, it is the only way that I know

To release the pains deep inside of me,

because now I feel invisible so there is no reason to continue to feel or ask, CAN YOU SEE ME?

COMPLETELY TIRED

Sick and tired of all your games and your lies

I am throwing up my hands with you now,

Some question why I allowed this much for so long.

And I cannot even begin to explain how.

The way that you treat other people, especially women.

Is so messed up, and I can no longer deal with your shit,

To some women, your actions may be cool with them.

But to me, it is f***** up and I am just not one of those chicks.

I am a woman, a mother, and a daughter.

And to you, I have been too good of a friend,

So rather than hate you, I have decided.

To go ahead on my way and put this between us to an end.

I do not know what you are used to.

But this treatment from you, I can and will no longer take,

Everything about you is built on lies and untruths.

Every part of you has turned out to be fake.

You will not sleep with me.

Then the next day or week with another,

My life and health are valuable to me.

Even if you choose to not care about your own, care for others.

Too many diseases going around.

And you are sleeping with her, and I unprotected,

I have never had to worry about becoming infected.

I am finished being nice to you now.

Going to treat you worse than you do, me,

I realize that you think I am just talking out of anger.

But this is a reality that I am going to make you see.

You do not deserve any part of me.

You have no respect for anyone else at all, and it is a shame,

What is even worse is that you

Play with people's hearts with all your bull**** ass games.

So, look, I am going to do you a favor.

And leave you alone to go ahead with them chick that you chose to lie for and sleep with,

And I am going to go ahead and begin my healing process.

I have given up on tolerating all your bullshit.

DADDY

I miss you, dad.

Wish that I had the chance to say,

The things that I did not get a chance to

Before you passed away.

I am the only one that did not get to talk to you.

And I wish that I would have known,

Because I would have said that I love you one last time

The night before and kept you on the phone.

If I could have seen, you the day that you left me.

I would have hugged you just to see your great big smile,

And I would tell you that I do not think.

That I could be without you, not even for a little while.

I did not get the chance to say a thing.

Not even a proper goodbye,

Although I am sure that you know this dad

It still hurts though; all I can do is imagine why.

You were gone so quickly.

And one last car ride alone you had to take,

And I know when you went to sleep that night.

You did not know that you would awake to heaven's gates.

GOD called your name.

So that you could come home, and enjoy heaven's beautiful things,

No more worrying or hurting for you.

All that was replaced with your wings.

Just wait up there in heaven for me

Please do not let me come alone,

The day that the angels come to get me.

Please, dad, be there first in line to bring me home.

FACE OF THE DEVIL

You said that I was deep, let's see how deep.

You think I am now, with the words I am going to speak to you,

The games that you are playing, did you know.

That this game needs a winner, so it is going to take two?

I am so sick of n****

I need to know if real men exist,

Because if they do, I will need to

Reup and redo the standards on my list.

You have encountered the right one.

Shawty, you have the eyes of the devil on your face,

But playing the games that you are trying to.

Is like a deck of playing cards, I am the spade, this game I have already aced.

You need to do your research.

And check my stats,

I am not bragging about myself.

Just for your well-being, I am stating the facts.

You pretend to be so different.

Yet you are just like the rest,

But unlike the other women, you run across

You have seemed to match up with the best.

You have the face of the devil.

Being deceitful and with all the games and lies,

And I will be damned if I allow another man.

To hurt me, let alone bring tears from my eyes.

Not another man, or anyone else

Is worth my time or heart's pain,

Before I allow you to stop me on this path

I will remove you from my life and lane.

Damn, I thought we were on the same page, and you would one day have my heart,

But now I see you are a liar like all others.

And cannot keep it real, even now, as you should've from the start.

So, I am going to go ahead and be on my way.

And give you more than your space,

So, you can play your games with someone else.

Because I am too good to play with anyone with the devil's face.

FEELINGS OF ANGER

Hate is such a strong word.

But I despise so many people, it is how I feel,

I have stopped caring for so many things.

My anger is so bad, that I think that I could kill.

I do not enjoy feeling this way.

Especially for loved ones or people I know,

That is why I stay to myself.

But some people have me so furious though.

I am tired of biting my tongue though.

And feeling as if I must kiss other's butts,

Tired of allowing my anger to stay inside.

And constantly build up.

I know if I am feeling like this.

That it is time for me to get away,

Find my circle of happiness.

And in that circle, allow me to stay.

People tend to always need me for things.

But if ever I need them, they are not there to help me out,

Some allow you to see new things.

And to finally see what they are about.

I have no one where I am now.

Everyone is out to get what they want from me,

They try to treat me badly or get me down.

Instead of pushing or supporting me to be what I can be.

Where I reside right now

Has my world so angry and uptight?

Yet all I want is to be happy again.

And make things in my life right.

I have so many negative thoughts at times

Wanting to delete people from my life,

Because a person cannot change for the better

If they keep negativity and misery in their life.

They say misery loves company.

I have come to see this to be true,

I see no use to keep doing for those.

That does nothing for you.

Beginning to turn back into how I used to be, so I will be treating folks as they do me.

Especially those trying to get me down,

I will start putting myself and mines first.

And it is how things shall remain here and now.

HATEFUL RAGE

How I am feeling right now is not a great feeling

I am feeling like I am in a jail or a cage,

All the hate that I feel for people.

Has me full of anger and rage.

I could say I just dislike them.

Cause they say hate is a word extraordinarily strong,

But hate is what I am feeling.

With those that I am among.

People, especially relatives can be cruel.

In this messed up world in which we live,

And all the shit people are doing to me now.

I will never forget, and as of right now I will never forgive.

I cannot stand people who are in my life.

Especially those that try to kick me down,

They need to realize and see that.

Their time will soon come around.

These are those, that more than I need them.

They tend to need me,

But I will no longer be there for them.

And this they are sure to see.

When people feel closed in and full of rage

They tend to eventually snap,

And then that level of sanity that they had

Will be hard to get back.

No one should ever get pushed to that point.

To ever feel the urge to kill,

I am losing all the love within me.

Because this is how they are making me feel.

I just need to get away from certain people.

From them, I need to get far away,

Because being in prison for murder

I do not wish to see that day.

I have worked hard in life to let go of hurt and rage.

From all the things that I have already been put through,

And I do not want to harm anyone so I will continuously pray.

To God to help me before I do.

I pray that I can get rid of this level of rage.

That is steadily growing back in my heart,

Had I 'd known this would happen?

Would have never stayed here from the start.

Sometimes I feel like a helpless bird.

That has been locked away in its cage,

I hope God grants me my wish to get away soon.

So that I can let go of this Hateful Rage.

VOICELESS VOICES: Words from a Broken Heart & Renewed Soul

HAVE YOU EVER?

Have you ever just sat and daydreamed?

Wishing that you could just fly away,

Or fly through life like a bird.

Not having to deal with the problems of today.

Have you ever felt that you love someone so much?

To the point that their words make you cry,

Making you feel like just giving up on them.

And no longer wanting to try?

Have you ever wondered?

Where it is that you would be if, you had made a different choice,

Wondering if God is listening.

So that you could give him praise and rejoice?

Have you ever felt like just giving up?

And letting everything go,

Just allowing all your emotions to come out.

Not caring if they show.

Has anyone had others come into their lives?

Where all they do is tear you down,

And you just accept it.

Because you think it is true love that you have found?

Have you ever had someone that you think that you love?

Come off to the point of being too aggressive,

They have you thinking that they love you as well.

Yet it turns into something possessive?

Has anyone ever felt that no matter what?

And no matter how right you tend to act,

It seems like it does not pay to move forward.

Because you are always knocked double the steps back?

Have you ever felt like?

You are going through too much unnecessary stuff,

Felt like you had all that you can take.

And that you been had enough?

INFIDELITY

I am not a strong believer in once a cheater always one.

I believe that you can stop and get better,

Some seem to feel that if you do it once.

That you will remain that way forever.

I believe that if two people have a bond.

There are many things together that they can achieve,

There will be obstacles they can get over together.

They can beat all the odds if they trust and believe.

You must know exactly where you are headed.

Trust in your companion and know who they are,

Believe in yourself as well as them.

Having faith in your relationship will allow you to go far.

Having faith in who you are is important.

Trusting in your significant other is the first step,

Keeping things only between you two

And making sure all promises, and secrets are kept.

Some people choose to go out and cheat.

When they are not happy anymore,

I have always wondered why we continue.

To remain in the relationship for.

Nowadays, rather than cheat on me.

I would rather they just leave,

Instead of remaining around to end up hurting me.

And constantly figuring a new way to deceive.

Infidelity causes people amounts of hurt and pain they cannot go forward from

The pain is too much to bear for some,

Then you have others who try to hurt you in return

Then that Is when all the games come.

They say what is done in the dark

Will one day come to the light,

And when it is too late, you realize.

That two wrongs do not make a right.

LIFE

My, greatest inspiration used to be my greatest motivation. Now, all she is it seems is the one quickest to break me down, and out to destroy my, determination. What I always thought to be the greatest gift in my life, is the one causing me more pain, more stress, and surely more strife, in my life.

LIFE- she is supposed to be my motivation. My biggest audience, the one who is supposed to be with and beside me through it all, cheering me on from the stands. But the pain and hurt she is causing me with the lack of respect she gives me seem to have crushed me worse than any man.

LIFE- why is life so hurtful, so full of disappointments, that thing that has me feeling like, my goals of greater things I should no longer strive to achieve, this is a part of life I could never have imagined or believed. I have given up more with and for LIFE, than I thought of or dreamed as a child that I ever would, but life has been out to knock me down as much as she could. At least with a man, the hurt is what you would expect, but with LIFE, this hurt, honestly, I would never expect. Yeah, I know, you are thinking or saying to yourself, Life is hard as hell, it will knock you down, pick you up, and we go through all types of shit in life, the good, the bad, and the ugly, right? Especially in situations but this thing I call life is not just any relationship.

I have been her greatest inspiration, always pushing her to do her best and letting her know I got her back and will always be here, preparing her for the outside world, keeping her safe, and ensuring that she can achieve whatever she feels she deserves, so for me to get in return what I have from LIFE, I really cannot believe that she has the nerve.

LIFE! Hmmm, LIFE, what is life for you? Does Life love us, does love exist at all within LIFE? LIFE has shown me lately, so much disrespect and, ways of deceiving. But I suppose with my luck in life, it was what within me, she was set out to be achieving. Damn, LIFE. Is it even worth going on, or waiting and wanting a change within LIFE? I just want to give up and walk away from LIFE, I no longer want this part of My life within me to live. How can I even think of a better way if I cannot even figure out if LIFE, I will ever be able to forgive?

LIFE!

MISTREATED

Decided to take it back to the basics.

And drop the nice and kind approach,

Decided to begin treating people worse than first-class plane riders.

Feel when they are sat back in coach.

They say do unto others as you would.

Want to be done,

Yet my tolerance level for bullshit now

Is at less than zero to none.

I am so finished playing the nice girl now.

My heart will now be ice cold,

And the love and kindness that was in my heart.

Are now on reserve and hold.

Like the old music group Allure

My eyes are "All Cried Out,"

Or damn near close to it, my tears are dried up.

Leaving my heart with so many doubts.

Life has brought me to the point.

Of starting to live life heartless, with no emotions,

And all due to all of those who mistreated me.

Now caused my doubt about men, with me constantly coming up with my assumptions.

Tried to give another one my time.

My heart and a part of me,

But he has shown me his true self much sooner than the last

Had no time to cover my eyes, I see.

These men are so used to mistreating women.

So, they tend to lose focus or their eyesight,

Of a good women's worth

Once she walks into his life.

Talking to and treating me bad

Is truly something that I refuse to tolerate?

I refuse to allow another man to tear me down.

What he had no part in helping to create.

I know my value and my worth

And most of all, I know exactly what I deserve,

Men seem to not realize it, or they do not care.

Then wonder why I act nonchalantly with my heart on reserve.

Hope to one day meet a man.

Who knows how to be loyal and true

Knows how to treat women with respect,

And realize that strong women know.

Just how much we are willing to accept.

Treat me as you would want someone to treat.

Your daughter or your mother,

Speak to me with the respect that I give you.

Because what you do not give to me, believe I will get it from another.

Mistreating the one who genuinely cares for you.

It Will only hurt you in the end,

She will one day give up and step away.

Leaving you wondering, how, why, what, and when.

So, sit back, reflect, and realize what you have.

Because trust me, she will get fed up with how you talk to her too,

And a lack of respect could be one thing.

That makes her finally pack up and do what she needs to do.

She cares a lot for you, but the way you do her.

Shows that you want it to be over,

If that is the case, just be real and say what you need.

And give both of you, your closure.

MY CLOSURE

How can you tell your child that you hate them?

And that you don't love them anymore,

This is something that you will always have to live with

It will make your child's heart forever be sore.

If you tried to apologize and turn back the hands of time

I think it would be too late,

And being me, I would like to know

Why for me, do you feel so much hate?

You have many downfalls mom,

But they are downfalls that I tried to accept

Because you are my mother, I tried to forgive you

And more than once, tried to make the first step.

You turned your back on us

You were the one who walked away,

You never cared enough to

Find out if your oldest child was even okay.

You allowed so many terrible things to happen to me

Sadly, you chose to love only one child, although he is my brother,

I must let you know that

You are a bad excuse for a mother.

You allowed your man to take my virginity as a child

And you took what was supposed to be a mother's love from my life,

Back at that age, it felt like through my heart

You stuck a knife.

I could never do to my child

The things that you have put me through,

I love my child unconditionally

The type of love that I never received from you.

You allowed me to get raped and physically abused

And to think, I was your oldest kid,

Now I have so much hate in my heart

Because of the things that you did.

I guess now, I have my closure

And can move on from my past

But as always all you care about is having a man,

I guess I will never know how a mother does this to her child

And I guess I will never understand.

NO TOLERANCE

Any unnecessary problems and drama

Life is just a little too short,

But just like an unwanted child

I wish these problems, I could abort.

If I wanted to deal with lies

I would still be with the last one,

But even with the love that I had for him.

My tolerance level dropped to none.

If I wanted to deal with disrespect

I had stayed with whom I took a vow,

But I left his ass alone as well.

As I am wanting to do now.

I am so tired of meeting all of these

Fake ass men, for real,

And them wasting my valuable time.

Or allowing them, my joy to steal.

These men that I am encountering nowadays.

Are sad excuses to me of a man,

They treat us women like shit seriously.

They pay us less attention than they pay to their clothing brands.

I want a man on top of their business.

Someone that is going to treat me as he would his mother,

Because if I am truly f****** with him

I am going to treat him with the level of respect that I would my son or my brothers.

I have a low tolerance.

For any dumb sh** from these men,

My tolerance level was much higher.

Back in the day, way back when.

So, listen, when you come at me.

Come correct, come whole, and come right,

Because if you are not ready or on my level

I will ignore you and ask you to get of out my sight.

My time is valuable.

And not here to be wasted on your disrespect,

Not only will I not tolerate it.

But there is so much that I am not willing to accept.

OVER & DONE

In the long run, trust

What you have done will hurt you, more than you hurt me,

Just sit back and wait a little while

And open your eyes, so that you don't miss it, you can see.

I gave you all my love, my whole heart

And you took all of it for granted,

And you will want me back someday

But it is a little too late because you didn't want It when you had it.

I gave you every part of me

But I am tired of fighting now, didn't have you as my own,

I guess you will realize that I am done when you look for me

And you realize this time there is no turning back, I am gone.

You know, for a while I wanted revenge on you

In any way, I could think of, but in a way you did it for me,

Because I know more now that from your lies and deceit

You helped me be free.

I am sure that you will try to talk to me, smile and come back

It never fails you always do,

You will see one day that I was the one woman

That remained loyal, loving, and of all else

Yet the one you chose to do these things to.

All your lying, cheating, drama

And on top of that, your days of deceit,

All I can do is pray to one day forgive you, but I thank you as well for helping me

To lock the revolving door and allow this chapter of my life to be complete.

PAINFUL EYES

Searching for something real

Everything seems so make-believe,

This life I am living seems.

Too much of a my-ste-ry.

I cannot keep smiling.

Acting and pretending as if everything is okay,

When underneath my smile is build up tears

That to myself, I let out when I am alone every day.

I give my all, my heart, all my love to

All the wrong ones in my life,

And I managed to break the heart of the one and only man.

He loved me more than anything and made me his wife.

My heart is so broken up right now, all over again.

And I do not know how to stop the tears from falling,

I should be smiling and happy.

And able to stop walking around with my smile hidden under this frown.

Why do I keep allowing myself this amount of pain?

So much of me has already been broken piece by piece,

No one loves me at all.

Or seems to care for me in the least.

I thought the last one hurt me.

And here I am again left with nothing, but my eyes watery red,

My heart was left hurt and empty.

Wishing my heart were dead.

Tried to believe someone else.

I tried to trust and love someone new,

But he turned out to be worse than the last

He ended up lying and hurting me too.

My pain allows me to keep me.

Loving him and hurting,

Constantly allowing him to break me.

And crying over a man not worth it.

What is it going to take for me?

To walk completely away,

And never turn around or look back.

Or speak again about this hurtful day?

All I can do now is lay here.

Staring up at my ceiling,

Crying my eyes out because of

The hurt and pain that I am feeling.

I just feel like, I am so ready to stop this hurt.

And I just want to shake off the feeling of wanting to die,

How do I bury my heart and heal this wound?

Because laying here right now, all I want to do is cry.

PATTERN OF LOVE

I continue to say how tired I am

But the truth is I have no idea of how to let go,

Don't even know how to move on

Or even if I can though.

His love and presence in my life have been all that I have known

Constantly for over the last 2 years,

I guess you can say that my being lonely forever now is

One of my greatest fears.

I swore that this time I had made up my mind

And that I was ready to move on,

The confusion is mostly because my love for him is still alive

But his actions toward me, show me his love for me has long gone.

I do not understand why I love this one so much

Or why do I keep allowing this pattern of love, pain, and hurt,

Why do I respect him so highly, and continue allowing him back in

Close enough and allowing him the ability to treat me with disrespect and like dirt.

I can say time in and time out that I know my value

Yet I keep allowing him to make me question my confidence and worth,

I fail to understand how anyone has the audacity

To think it is okay to hurt anyone else on this earth.

How can I expect to raise a daughter?

And to demand respect and something much better,

If I keep allowing her to see me accept from this man

What I do, and allow him to break me down consistently altogether?

How do I break off this line between love and hurt, and close the revolving door?

That I have tried to do in the past

They say all wounds heal with time and all,

But every time I am in the clear of my love for him

We make up again and I allow him in, to hurt me and make me fall.

Sometimes I wonder why the pain of love hurts so bad

And right now, there is so much of us that I miss,

But God I pray for you to please help me step over this line, and find the way to get out of this.

I am sick of all the lying, deceiving, and negativity, they are becoming too much for me to accept,

In my heart I know I still love him and always will

But I can no longer take any more games played with my heart, and his lack of respect.

STILL IN LOVE

I am still so in love with him.

So, I cannot allow myself to go into anything with another,

It would not be fair to the next person.

So, I must ask, why even bother?

I cannot say that I regret what I felt for him.

But I do miss him so much, this I must confess,

I feel like Kelly Rowland right now.

Because I am still so in love with my ex.

In my heart, the love I have was strong.

It still feels so real, he was like my best friend,

I can openly and honestly say that.

I never thought that we would ever end.

We were close to each other's families.

We did everything and anything together,

I always thought even if we were to stop messing around.

That at least we would remain friends forever.

Sometimes I must search my mind because I stay.

Questioning myself about what I did wrong, steady trying to figure it out,

Wondering if he ever loved and cared for me.

Because how he did me has me left with doubts.

Wondering how it was so easy for him.

To quit speaking to me out of the blue and move on to the next,

Yet it is so hard for me to do it at all.

Because I have so much love left in me for my ex.

I know that what I feel is real.

Although it does not seem to matter at all to you,

But I think that I would know the feeling of the love I feel, and if it's real or true.

I will surely get completely over him.

But for now, my heart shall remain locked and sealed,

I am a firm believer that I will be alright.

All wounds take time to be healed.

You know, although we began as just friends

That slowly turned into just sex,

We turned into a relationship, which was left with lies, hurt, and deceit.

That has left me partly scorned, yet still in love with my ex.

WITHOUT REMORSE

You used me, you lied to me, you tried your best to manipulate me

After I opened my home, my life, and tried to help you do what you said you wanted to,

I was the only one there for you when you needed someone

and I get disrespect, your ass to kiss, rejection, and more manipulation and bullshit from you.

You have some nerves, but I have reached my breaking point

You turned out to be much worse than any enemy

And turned out to be the worse type of man.

I do not understand why people we love treat us as they do

I will never get it; I will never understand.

I felt sorry for you, and you used stories like my past to pull me in.

I kept making excuses for your behavior and ignoring the red flags in front of my eyes,

Which only allowed you to continue pretending and manipulating me

With more of your empty promises and lies.

You did not want better for your life, wanted to continue doing the same things

With no remorse for who you hurt because you do not even love yourself

I am not sure how I expected you to care for, respect, or love anyone else.

I still tried to be there and to try to understand

But you were beginning to cripple my life,

I am the only one that I can honestly blame though

That you had the chance to stab me further in my back with your betrayal knife.

My intentions for helping you were nothing more than good

While your intentions for coming back into my life were nothing more than self-beneficial and bad,

You set out to destroy me and get all you could from me

And when your tactics couldn't get that, you decided to betray me with the only string that you had.

Doing wrong to the people that gave you a roof over your head when you were homeless, food in your mouth, water to wash with, and a warm bed,

Only for you to give me nothing in return besides more lies,

And an attitude for figuring out your bullshit, and all to me behind my back that you did.

You have not an ounce of remorse for the betrayal that you did to me

The one who allowed you to drown me consistently, yet I still tried to be there,

One of the only ones in your life who will tell you the truth about yourself

But still in it with you, and even with everything that happened, my heart still managed to care.

When you left my house, I told you that I would always be there

My door would always be opened if you should need me,

Only to find out more of your betrayal and deceit behind my back

I am guessing it was parts that you were hoping I would never find out or see.

You destroyed me, you destroyed the love in my heart and

The feelings of wanting to help another friend,

But I blame myself because I trusted you more than I should

I should have been seen through you from day one, but it's okay because the love for you from me has now come to an end.

You can never call me, reach out to me, or ever come back into my home

Let alone into my life or my space or my heart,

The betrayal you dished out to me with this last thing

Gave me back my power, my humility, my creativity, my wall, and my fight

I am still standing through this hurt, and the strength in me is stronger than it was from the start,

I am getting back up as Sarah Jakes said

I may have been scarred from you, but I am a child of the highest God,

I am a walking testimony. I am back fighting, and back knowing who I am when I look at myself,

You had me angry, ready to go back to the old spiteful, revenge-seeking me

But I have come too far to allow you to control me any further, and too far to allow you to stop me from loving or helping anyone else.

I will keep moving forward without your remorse, without your apologies

I am back up with a smile because I know who I was created to be,

The spirit that God has blessed my life with

Overflows with joy, high vibrations, love, growth, forgiveness, and the joys of embracing ME.

Without Remorse, I can admit, yes you cut me and

you betrayed me in the worst way,

I hope she was worth the short tears that you caused me, the one who had your back, but you, having access to me ever again, there will never be another day.

I am a victim of a true narcissist,

I hate to say it, but it is true,

You took my kindness as weakness, but never again will you have the chance

You have moved on, while you left me with a brief period of hurt and a soul that wanted to just shut down,

And to never again allow anyone in, let alone allow anyone around.

You are the definition of a FRIENEMY

The ones that Fab spoke about in his song "Frenemies"',

N***** wasn't with me,

They were just around me.

Everything that you did, you did it with a smile and WITHOUT REMORSE,

But I thank God for shining the light on exactly who you are

No hate for you in my heart, it takes too much energy, but my heart for you is empty now, it has taken a total change of course.

WOMAN FED UP

Told you before that my love had a limit

Now I have truly had it, I am fed up, there is nothing you can say or do,

When I tell you things you should pay attention.

It is too late now because of what we had been through.

See, I've tried everything to love and hold on

But I swear you change more than the seasons do,

One minute we are good and the next you pretend I have no feelings

As if I must accept BS and disrespect from you.

You need to sit and listen to the words in R. Kelly's "When A Woman's Fed up" Song

Because it's like I've always said, ALL men are the same,

The only difference between them is the name.

I am an independent, strong, woman

Raised not to depend on or trust many anyway,

This time I may cry a little and miss us

But believe me when I tell you, I will make it without you in my way.

It is so confusing to me, why women give men so much of ourselves

Then they make us go through so much bs in return,

But you know, even with the men that claim to love us

Eventually, that flame blows out and it of course leave a burn.

I am so fed up now seriously, though

I may forever love you, it is a fact,

But your love and respect for me I am uncertain of

My only certainty as of now is that the time I gave you, I will never get it back.

You treat me worse than shit at times

I wonder who told you that, that was ever cool,

They say only fools fall in love

But I am sick and tired of playing your fool.

Answer me this though:

Do you see my strength? Do you know I love you because I choose to? Do you ever think that I get fed up? Do you know my value and worth, or do you ever think I get tired of all the lies?

Well, what you know or think no longer matters

Because I am that Woman fed up

So now I am going to go ahead and move on and say goodbye.

WOMAN SCORNED

Wondering why I am lately feeling like Letoya

And feeling confused and torn,

Walking around full of anger

Looking like a woman scorned.

Black clouds surrounding my heart and soul

As if I were stuck in a hurricane,

The rising tides ever so high

As I keep hearing someone calling my name.

My tears slowly filling up into a puddle

But to listen not a single sound,

And marking their path of what is to be

A raindrop coming down.

For today has been cast upon me

More hurt and nothing to protect me from harm,

And everyone that I think loves me, has betrayed me

There is that ringing sound in my ear again, but it is just the sound of hurt sounding the alarm.

The white clouds quickly turn black

Showing the thin line between love and hate,

Allowing me to see the one person hurting me

Is the face of my lifetime mate.

I used to be so alive,

But others set out to leave me scorned,

Made me wish at times that

I was never born.

All these years I have been hurting

For so many reasons, carrying it around undercover,

Ended up on this road of love again

Now being hurt by my husband and lover.

I am tired of meeting all the wrong people

Tired of hearing the words I am sorry,

But without times of pain

How would I be able to tell my story?

I tried to take on the task

In playing the good wife,

I thought it was my time to settle down

And deem a new purpose in life.

Praying to one day let of the scornful parts of my world

And be around those without hurtful intentions,

Someone that has a real level of respect and a mind of their own

Instead of needing validation and to live up to society's conventions.

I need someone in my life

That will play a major role,

Someone who will do right by me

And will keep me in his mind, body, and soul.

Now, I have told another story

Of bitter love, which has left my heart disappointed,

And I've been trying to steer away from those

Who leaves my heart feeling unanointed?

So, I ask you to bring on and use all your resources

And a dream that roses adorn,

Because most enjoy happiness and real love

Instead of becoming a WOMAN SCORNED.

SECTION III: SOUL RENEWED

"Noone rises to low expectations"

Les Brown

A WOMAN'S WORTH

SHE is a significant other, someone's wife.

A daughter, a niece,

A leader, a coach, an activist, a writer, a voice. SHE bares life.

SHE is a mother, an entrepreneur, a dreamer, an aunt, a sister, and a friend.

SHE is a survivor, a conqueror, someone who continues to get back up

SHE keeps fighting until the end.

SHE cares for everyone around her

But no one asks her about her day or supports her dreams.

Who even cares,

So-called loved ones use and abuse her kindness,

SHE feels lonely most days, and her tears to others are as invisible as the air.

SHE cooks, SHE works, SHE hustles

SHE does everything to live her life and enjoy the time she has to,

SHE comforts others, SHE laughs, and she manages to know how to hide her pains sometimes

To be able to be there, uplift, and inspire others to get through.

This is all SHE IS, and what does she receive in return?

Betrayal, deceit, disrespect, hurt, tears, and days of her feeling depressed,

More pain, more lies, no support, and keeping her stressed.

SHE has been tortured. SHE has been raped. SHE has been abandoned. SHE has been abused,

Folks have set out consistently to deceive her and leave her hurt and used.

SHE will swallow her pride

And put all her feelings to the side.

To ensure someone else is taken care of, they are good,

But a second thought on her well-being, who would?

You talk about her, call her names like Lady, Bitch, Stupid, Worthless, nobody, or SHE,

But she has a name, and there are better ways to describe her,

Her worth means much more than what you give credit for, she means much more to people like Me.

SHE takes her pain and trials and makes something out of it.

Standing on the visible cuts in her back, pulling out the knife

And SHE stands up strong and tall

dries her eyes again and continues moving on in her life.

SHE never forgets, but she learns to forgive

Yes, you call her all those negative names, but I call her:

Beautiful, Survivor, Fighter, Conqueror, Strength, Gifted, Talented, LOVE, A CHILD OF GOD, POWERFUL, THE VOICE, and WORTHY WOMAN!

BROTHER

I Always wondered about the man that

I would watch from a distance to grow,

Wondered why I have never been close to you

Only for a brief period, of you, did I know.

Although we have never really been close

You have always been on my mind and in my heart,

Especially once you went away again

And the little bond we managed to build, for some reason we grew apart.

We've both had hard lives growing up

But you were a special part of my life, I felt you from within,

Sometimes I sit and reminisce on our fun time.

And wonder how our lives could have been.

Things within myself and with you, I blame myself for

Thinking about your life, I sit here trying to stop these tears,

I have searched for answers to the questions that have

Gone unanswered for so many years.

I am not the perfect person at all, but I have done well for myself

Although for some reason you feel I am a bad sister to you,

But it hurts more not knowing why you feel like this

And I do not even have the slightest clue.

Growing up you know what I endured.

And how it has grown with me, but it no longer affects me today,

And although our parents were not there our whole lives, especially for you

To an extent they created the path for us to find ourselves in our way.

We can never turn back the hands of time

But you are my brother, and I love you and hope we can

Grow together even at a distance on this fresh new road,

Let go of and forgive one another from our past

As we watch our new lives created and unfold.

Baby brother, I just want to say that I apologize.

And hope you understand and know that I do love you,

and want you to know that I will always be there

and hoping vice versa that you will always be here for me too.

I am sorry for all the anger from the hurt that you had to endure

along with the continuous pattern of trauma, anger, and pain,

I am sorry you cannot get back all that you have lost in life

But take it from me, look at your family and appreciate and realize the good that you gained.

I need you to take the advice that I give to you

And decide to let go of the past, change your life, and just forgive,

Know that you are doing it for yourself and not them

So, you can clear your mind, and finally no longer just exist, but be able to LIVE.

Create a greater you and understand you have a purpose for your life

Break the chains of trauma left on you by our father and mother,

Make your dreams a reality, use your story, and believe that this time you will succeed

Although you are not perfect and will make more mistakes, just know that I got you, my brother.

CONNECTED FOREVER

We may not end up together forever when it is all said and done

But it is no secret that our souls are forever connected, through the permanent growth that together we have earned,

And the moments that we spent together throughout our term

Are mixed with all the things in life together that we have grown through, shared, and learned.

The person that I have become and grown into today

Is partly because of you,

Just as the person and woman you have grown to learn and be

Is partly because of the role that I played in your life, too.

Our feelings have never changed for each other,

Although we sometimes may need our own space,

But the place in my heart that you have is forever

It can in no way ever be replaced.

Not everything we do is perfect

And not everything we say will be right, sometimes things may come out through anger and be wrong,

But the time has proven repeatedly that the love that we share

Will forever stay strong.

We are a part of each other

A real and true sacred bond we do share,

Not having you in my life to call on or speak to ever again

Is a pain that I could never see myself having to bare.

Meeting you was not by mistake, it was for a purpose

This is a fact of truth that I know,

God placed us into one another's lives at the right time

To heal one another but also to grow.

There is a purpose to our meeting and being who we are together and separately

There is a greater purpose in us continuing together in this untold story,

There is a purpose for us to travel the journey that we are on of fantasy,

A world and a life that is unknown to us on where we will end up together

But it is a journey worth taking if we both believe

Knowing that no matter what, we will end up happy and fulfilled, together.

Even if we do not end up together for life as we planned

Our souls will forever be tied together until life forever closes the curtain,

This love we share is real even through the ups and down

That not even the devil can come between, this I know for certain.

Your name is forever on me, but also

Forever tattooed on my heart,

And nothing and no one in life will be able

To rip our souls apart.

FINDING YOURSELF

Through anger, rebelling, temporary fixes, hurtful words to those closest to you,

You try to escape and deny your depression,

But there is no hiding or running from

Your true and real reflection.

Because as you continue to try to ignore things or run away

The reflection of you and your life gets nearer,

And instead of changing yourself

You try to change the mirror.

But ask yourself, what will you do when the mirror you look in

Eventually falls down,

What do you do when that mirror breaks into pieces

And it hits the ground?

Listen, the obstacles, bad choices, struggles, and pain that you endured are not who you are,

For you are not your file,

But you must tell yourself this and believe it

And decide that your past journey, now has you on a new one, with greater steps and extra miles.

Change is scary, and finding out just who we are is even more full of fear

But fear can and will be only as bad as you allow your mind to imagine it,

It is not as much about the obstacles within your life

But more so about how you choose to handle it.

You are still here, in today's world God has given you another chance

Not only to make things right but to live and to find out just who you were designed to be and what it is you are supposed to do,

Stop worrying about things you cannot change

And only focus on the things that you can change within and for yourself.

Stop hurting others who God placed into your life

Because one day they will give up, and when you realize it, it will be too late,

For you to mend things between you because of your words and ways

Turned their love and respect for you, from love to hate.

Life is something unfortunately none of us can fake

But we live and we learn from each mistake.

Stop taking life for granted as if we have forever to live or mend relationships

Or apologize for things or to people we hurt, that our pain dished out,

Never getting the chance to let them know

That the words spoken to them that hurt them, doing that intentionally was not what it was ever about.

Your hurt is important, your trauma and mistakes do not determine who you are

Your past is just that, your past,

But stop making the same choices, and live moments as if they were your last.

It is easier said than done, this I know, but

All your sadness, anger, limitations, distractions, and pains

Let it flow upstream, wash it away like rain.

Look at yourself in that mirror that stares back at you

And see what you can be, and be glad that the mirror still stands firm, and be happy that when

That last one fell, you did not cut yourself, with the mirror's glass,

And realize, know, and understand that the hardest times in your life

Are behind you, the toughest battles you have defeated, they have passed.

This time when you look in the mirror at yourself

Choose to look with open eyes,

So that you can see what others see when they look at you

And if you do not like the outside of what you see, you can choose then, to look on and update the inside.

I WANT TO KNOW YOU

I am not interested in what you do for a living

Or what you have done in your past

Instead, I want to know what you ache for

And if you ever dream of what your heart longs to see.

I want to know if you would be willing to risk

Looking like a fool for the love of a woman that

Has your back through it all or if you will risk

Looking like a fool to make your dreams a reality

And for the love of being alive.

I am not interested in you not being perfect.

I want to know if you have ever touched on the center of your pain deep inside

Or if you have ever been betrayed by someone you love. I want to know if you have been closed off from the fears of further pain.

I am not interested in rather or not the stories and words that you are telling me are all true or if they have all been filled with lies.

I want to know if you can disappoint another to be true to me. I want to know if you are willing to disappoint another human being to be true to yourself.

I need to know if you can be trustworthy and true.

I am not interested in only the ugly part of your heart and soul. I want to know if you can see the beauty in life. If you can see the beauty in what I share with you and see it in my visions when I look at you. I want to know that you can see the beauty of things, even when everything in life is not so pretty every day and you can source your own life from it.

I want to know if you can live with the failures of both of us, and still stand tall to the ends of the earth and have high vibrations and belief in knowing things will get better and change and blessings will flow when you are ready to allow GOD in.

I do not care to know how much money you have, or how much money you can make in the fast life. I want to know that after a night of grief, you can get up, stand tall and keep pushing forward.

I am not interested in who you know. I am interested in knowing if I Had to stand in the fire, that you would stand with me and not turn your back on me.

I am not interested in who you have been with before me. I am interested in knowing what sustains you from the inside out. I am interested in knowing where you would like to see your life in the next 3-5 years. I am interested in knowing how you will get there. I am interested in knowing can you see yourself loving yourself. I am interested in knowing YOU and helping you know you too.

I want to know if you can be alone with yourself and if you are okay with the company that you keep when you are alone within your real thoughts? ME? My interest is in getting to know the real YOU!

LIVE LIFE

Life is short this we all know, so please Live and cherish each moment you are given

And feel with your heart all that you can,

Cherish the life you have been given with all it is worth

Just as I do. My purpose in life is all that I am.

Face head-on the blessings coming your way

And release any hesitance or fear,

See those God placed in front of your eyes to help you

For that vision alone is crystal clear.

Embrace the moments God has given you again

Do not allow them again to slip away,

For tomorrow is not promised so stop putting off till tomorrow or later

What it is you can do today.

You cannot turn back the hands of time

Or change someone else,

But you can choose a better life and make the necessary changes now

for your personal growth, as you learn how to love and forgive yourself.

What happens in our lives sometimes, we will never really understand.

You can no longer allow yourself to continue to get caught up in the negative, instead be happy with the second chance at life that you have been given,

Live for today, for today is before you

Choose to get up, start moving and of course start living.

You cannot fix the past at all

The past is the past for a reason, it is now gone,

It can no longer be changed, for it is unchangeable

It has passed and for the greater of self, choose instead to move on.

You must open your heart and allow God to change you, and your thoughts

But to learn the lessons for you that life has in store,

You must humble yourself in more than just your words

And choose to place fear of failure aside, by choosing to open new doors.

Stop being afraid to try something new,

Because with each new experience you allow for yourself

There is a new benefit and blessing for you.

Life passes us by so quick, so fast

and one life is all that we get,

Stop taking life for granted, only to someday look back with a life full of regrets.

MY ANGEL NOW

If you should see my angel in heaven, his name is Papa

He will not be hard to find,

He will be the one cooking fish or fishing for more

He is one of a kind.

He will be the one with the baseball cap

Placed halfway on his head,

Or he will be eating Jell-O and playing chess

Telling of old and long stories of all the things that he did.

My Papa will be sitting with all the storytellers

Because besides being my Papa, a great dad, and fishing, telling stories is what he did best,

He was not perfect, but he gave life his best

Until God saw him tired and called him home to rest.

Now if you have yet to spot my Papa,

It is probably because he is praying with God for all of us down below,

Cheering us on and proud to see the lives we live

And how each of us continues to grow.

When you do see my Papa in heaven

Please let him know that I have graduated college and work in the medical field, and I am doing fine,

Let him know that I love and miss him

and he is in my heart forever, and he is close beside me all the time.

My papa was my hero, my very first best friend, the man who showed me true love

Please for me give him a hug or two,

Tell him it is from his Baddy thing

And that I am the one who sent you.

SOUL RENEWED

My life has grown so much within the years

My spirit has been renewed and healed,

My voice was stolen from me at an early age

No longer shut and sealed.

I am like a phoenix rising from the ashes

My spirit and life have been rebirthed, and I stand strong,

It feels great, I must admit

My voice was quiet for far too long.

My voice has now been amplified

I have been evolving in every aspect of life,

God has shown me so many things lately

and gave me the means to live out my purpose-driven life.

My soul was broken into pieces one too many times

But God stitched it back together,

He helped me forget the pains and betrayal from my past

And to accept who he said that I was and to love myself better.

My feet slowly have been moving in all the right directions

Moving past the times where my heartfelt unaligned,

Going through the hurt seasons in my life to where I am now

In this new journey of life, the directions have now been shown and defined.

I feel more than renewed now that the sting from those cuts has dissolved

After pouring into me all those pains,

My blood finally flowed again from the words

Of my poetry, rhyming like music throughout my veins.

I walk today feeling alive and free

From all that was there to destroy and destruct parts of me.

My body and mind have finally washed away all the shame and fear,

Life was supposed to end long ago, but because of God, I am still here.

Still fighting, finally living, and loving myself

Now able to allow myself to be loved and give love to someone else.

I am a new me, a greater me, a better me, a renewed and strengthened me,

For today, God resides inside of me.

God showed up, and his light shined through,

Cured my broken heart and mended my soul, my spirit now renewed.

I opened my eyes to a new dawn,

I allowed the dark places of my past to fade finally,

I prayed continuously to forgive until the pain was gone and my voice could be heard

And I no longer felt afraid.

Time for me to continue this growth road I am on

And continue to heal every day, I will not lose my fight,

I am opening new scrolls now and focused on my goals

Because God promised me everything would be all right.

I am holding on to happiness, love, success, purpose, passion, confidence, strength, and so much more now

The betrayal, deceit, lies, shame, pains are part of my past

They are my testimony and my story that many can relate to

A story that I can write and share at last.

I am taking off the shelf any negativity and focusing on my new direction

It is all about this new journey that I am on and what it has yet to come,

My life is what I make of it, and I am proud of who I have become.

SPIRITUAL SOLITUDE

Have you ever been in a room full of people?

Yet feel so alone,

Feeling constantly trapped in a solitary zone?

With laughter and smiles that never seem to last

Because painful memories and regrets resurface from your past.

Suicide is the easy answer for me, my way out

Multiple times I have tried,

To leave this world full of hate and chaos

That takes over my temporary happiness and replaces it with the tears that I have cried.

Hoping and praying that I can get through the demonic thoughts taking over my mind and body

But hope is all an illusion, a prediction,

My mind is so clouded, that I can no longer distinguish or understand

What is real and what is fake and fiction.

Hell, and heaven, for me, seems like fair game,

My question to myself is, will I overcome by succumbing to peace

or will I fall forever in shame?

Here I am again in a room full of people yet feeling alone

Trapped in this solitary zone.

I try to get away to feel better or to hide my tears and all,

But every way I turn, there seems to be some type of wall.

Depression continues to move on in,

And my only weapon against it is my pad and my pen.

Loneliness consumes me; it eats away the years

Until my life is swallowed by unending fears.

God, I need you,

I cannot do this on my own

You are the only one who knows

Where my fears are sewn.

I am tired of hiding up under this mask

pretending to be happy or someone else,

I need your help, I need

to find myself.

As of today, I am still here, I could be dead,

Thank God though, I have conquered it, I have survived,

So, trust me, you can and will get through this

With Your goal to not give up and to fully recover

It will manage strongly to keep you alive.

Please DO NOT GIVE UP. If you or someone you know is suicidal or battling depression, please contact me at khalilahhpurnell@gmail.com . or contact the suicide hotline at 1-800-273-8255. YOUR LIFE MATTERS!

THE PRESENCE OF GOD

I remember someone asking me a while back

How I know God is present, he is real,

They questioned how I believed that something unseen

I explain more about the reasons why I feel as I feel.

So many questions about the presence of our higher being

Because of all the bad happening in the world around us,

Many questions on how I can put in a being unseen

My undying or unquestionable trust.

God created us all with a plan for each of us

From the time we were created, on the very first day.

Though sad and Frustrating times will be,

But someday we all open our hearts and see life in God's way.

We all have a story to tell, journeys we all traveled through

We each have scars, and because of GOD, my scars tell

of how the things that I went through and now I have overcome,

if not for the presence of God in my life, I would not have made it through

of all the things from which I have come.

My scars show and tell a story, that none would believe if I was not here still standing to tell

My scars used to be silent, they barely whispered about the pains that I faced,

But now my voice is amplified in confidence, and I can share it with you

About the marathons that I raced.

Because of God, my scars can now speak louder

They can tell a story of something so much greater,

The story that I have been given to share with the world

About the presence of our Creator.

Allow my story, my words, my life to be your voice, your belief

That things do get better, you do conquer the things meant to destroy you, you no longer must allow them to control you anymore,

God is very much present with you throughout your battles

Showing you how he will lift you through them, and on his wings, you will soar.

My past could be like yours and I want you to proclaim

That all things work together for good,

Thinking back there is no way I could have gotten through the things I endured by myself

But with the presence of God, I did. And you need to know, you will, and you could.

So please look, even in the unseen, the unknown,

Feel in your heart what you know is real, feel his presence in you and see

That GOD is real! His love and his presence prove over and over

Through the trials of life that I traveled on the journey, my growth and survival point to him, not me.

I need no photos to prove the real presence of GOD

To hang upon my wall.

I do not need a portrait,

or for non-believers, His presence to recall.

For those who wish to listen to the truth and my testimony, many of ours are similar

It is played throughout the land.

The symphony of life itself,

Directed by God's hand.

TRUE FRIEND

I found a special and devoted friend recently.

Who knew all that I felt?

She knew all my weaknesses.

And every problem I had been dealt.

She understood my thoughts.

And listened patiently to my dreams,

She even listened to my thoughts on life.

And knew what all of it means.

Not once did she interrupt while I spoke.

Or even try to say that my feelings were wrong,

She understood all that I was going through.

And promised to be by my side all along.

She always helps me if I should fall

She Motivates and inspires me

And answers me if I should call.

Confronts me and tells me when I am wrong

But in the same way, this devoted friend shows me my strength and keeps me strong.

When tears or fear creep in, she knows the words to say to

Make the fears, dripping eyes, and stagnancy go away,

and just like the sun, she brightens my day.

She sees things in me that I do not see in myself sometimes, and sometimes I may deny,

And she spreads for me, my wings to fly.

Just like a book, my mind she reads,

And offers me, at the right time the things that I need.

How, can I ever repay this special friend?

I managed to extend my hand to reach out to this friend.

To show my appreciation and how much I care,

Tried to pull her closer to let her know.

That I appreciate her being there.

I went to hold her hand.

So that I could pull her nearer,

And I realized this devoted friend that I found.

Was nothing but a mirror!

WHAT IT MEANS TO LOVE

To love is to build and share a life

To work together through everything side by side as two,

Smiling and learning about life, one by one, as one

While together we make our dreams come true.

To love is to encourage and empower one another

through the smiles and the tears, day by day,

as we take time to listen and care

in many affectionate and tender-hearted ways.

To love is to share life with that special someone

Who, no matter what you can always depend,

Who will be there and protect you

As your partner, lover, and friend.

To love is to make memories that last a lifetime

That you can look back and smile and see the growth at the moment you enjoy being able to recall,

Of all the things you went through together

LOVE is the greatest of it all.

I have learned in this lifetime the true meaning of love

As life continues to show and teach me new things, as my dreams are beginning to come true,

I have learned the true meaning of love and being in love

When I learned to love myself, and as I learned to love you.

WHEN I LOOK AT YOU

My only born, my first blessing besides life itself

The love I have for you is the love I never dreamed I would be able to give to anyone else.

The feeling I felt the first time I saw you, is the same feeling I get when I look at you now and see your smile.

The first time you placed your tiny fingers into mine,

I knew then this was a love that could never be replaced

A love like no other, my heart was yours until the end of time.

I have watched you throughout the years, laugh, cry, hurt, and grow,

And the hardest part of these feelings is knowing that one day in life one of us will have to let the other go.

I may be hard on you at times or things I say may come across as harsh or unfair,

But the tough love or advice I give sometimes is because I am a flawed parent, but I love you and I care.

But no matter how old you get or no matter the miles of where you may be,

You have someone rooting for the best for you, and that someone is me.

I ask God to continuously watch over you and to always protect you, baby girl

From everything set out to destroy you within this dark-filled world.

Daughter- I wish that you could see what I see when I look at you.

You possess a beauty, confidence I used to be jealous of,

One that no one can ever deny,

If you could see what I see when I look at you

You would fall in love with yourself and forever hold your head up high.

I need you to see what I see when I look at you,

So, you could know and see that there is nothing that you cannot do.

I need you to see what I see when I look at you

And allow any insecurities that you may have or anger or shame, go,

I need you to believe in you as I believe in you, and

Hold your head up and never allow your crown to fall,

For you are a strong black Queen, who can reach all levels that you choose to as you continue through life within to grow.

I need you to see what I see when I look at you

I see a young woman whose smile could brighten up the darkest night,

I apologize now if my grip around you seems to be too tight.

I see in you, A young woman filled with love, confidence, accomplishments, and visions, dreams and goals as you move and evolve to new levels and heights, and I am sorry for being

a mother that loves her child too hard sometimes, not allowing you to make your mistakes and your own decisions.

I see A mature woman, filled with mixed emotions, still learning herself

Learning what makes her happy and not needing to depend on anyone else.

I wish that you could see what I see when I look at you

I see your arduous work, your dedication, and your efforts,

That will someday add up to what you desire to achieve, trust me you will see,

That all that you have prayed for and believed in will come to fruition and that

The incredible and successful woman that you know that you are destined to be.

I must now learn to sit back gently and trust God to continue to protect you from harm

As I allow you to live your life and let you continue to grow,

And realize that I must loosen my grip on you because you are your own woman, and you need me to live my own life and seek to let go.

I will not let go completely, but I promise to gently loosen my grip,

Just know I will be here for you forever just in case you slip.

I am now signing off from this poem daughter. I love you

More than you could ever know,

Remember forever that no matter what

Your mother will never let you completely go.

I need you to see what I see when I look at you,

You are a diamond that shines brightly

That diamond in the rough that I will always call my little girl,

you are mine,

I hope that you can see what I see when I look at you,

Which is, that God made my Diamond Shine!

YOU

YOU! See, you think there is a different version of You.

Some that are, better than other parts of you.

But the Version you are in right now, is, the one that you never thought that you wanted to be, right? Well, let us get to the root of that....

I see- A deeper you. I see YOU. The whole you.

Not the segmented versions of you, and I like what I see- in YOU!

See- I created You, in completion. I made the complete YOU, the true you.

YOU- With all your mistakes, hurts, traumas, fears, regrets, and second chances. YOU....

The You that is fighting a never-ending battle in your mind that says that.

Letting go of the idea that there is a better version of you just around the corner waiting to be realized or created. Or that the better version of you is in the past, when you were stronger or younger, and had the entire world ahead of you, that is the you that you want to believe is a different and better version of self. But I am here to tell you, that the old version of you, is still you, it is just you in a greater form per se,' but it is still you, just a renewed you where your eyes are wide open to realize just who you are. The beauty in you. The strength that comes with you. YOU!

I am here to help you see who I see when I look at you. What do I see right now is the entire-not just a portion of you? Do you see who I see when you look at yourself?

Let me show you- exactly who- you are. Let me help you see you. Let me help you hear you. Let me help you love you. Let me help you trust you. Let me help you-embrace you. YOU!

Do not allow another to define your worth or value. You are worthy. You are significant. Only focus on who I say that you are. Look at you in the mirror. That person looking back at you-and smiling in a loving and encouraging way-is the true YOU. LOVE YOU.

Self-love is like a science and a revolution that every atom inside of your body should be marching for.

Take a second to finally open your ears and your heart to listen to YOU. Living your life forgiving yourself and knowing that you are loved will be what makes you abandon regrets, and you that seem to look for another version of you to surface or shine through. Look deeper...... inside of your soul and see YOU! Never stop loving YOU!

Accept all your flaws, truths, and your past. Make peace with who- you are and where you have been. YOU- are so much more than what you give yourself credit for.

Adore you. Bet on yourself. Believe in yourself. Speak life into the person you see every day in that mirror. You are POWERFUL. Still the same you, just renewed. Still standing- created by the energy of the universe itself. YOU! YOU ARE LIFE!

THE MEANING OF A BLACK DIAMOND. YOU ARE- POETRY OF… YOU!

THANK YOU!

I want to say thank you again to our creator. GOD, you designed this gift. You blessed me to be able to grow within my writing and other areas of my life during the waiting process of growing my writing. This is the assignment that you ordained and gave me to put out first, and it is just what we together ensured took place. I just want to say thank you. Thank you for my journeys in my life. Thank you for not allowing my first passion to dissolve, but instead to evolve. Thank you for confirming so many things that I already felt and knew, through visions, words, and gifts that I now understand. Thank you in advance for what is to come and the lives that this book will bless, heal, give a voice to and bring understanding to.

Secondly, I thank my daughter. You have shown me some lessons in my life that I didn't know before giving birth to you. You have shown me a love outside of the love from God that I never knew existed. Even through all our trials and tribulations, and your feelings toward me for my mistakes as a woman, lessons were learned, some in the past and many in the present by the grace of God. We have had our ups and downs, but I would not trade you for another child or being in the world. I love you with my entire soul and I am so proud of the woman that you are and are consistently turning into. Thank you for loving me FOR ME, flaws and all.

I also want to say Thank you to my daughter from another mother, Shaneyea Conwell. Woo, where do I begin? I will just say this, you are an incredible young woman, and I thank you from my entire heart for loving my daughter. You and I have come a long way to being where we are with our relationship, but as time and life shift, so do we as individuals. You have watched me grow and I have watched you grow as well, and GOD continues to grow each of us separately in life. I thank you for pouring into me. I thank you for being a part of my audience with my books. I thank you for the tears and passion while listening to many of my words. Keep being who you are, while changing the parts of you that God needs you to and always trust GOD.

I thank also my Pastor of Colossian Baptist Church, Pastor Peter A. Evans and the first lady, Cheryl Evans, as well as the deacons, deaconess, minister, and the congregation for all of your help and assistance when I needed you all the most. I thank Pastor for never turning your back on me, always praying for me and mines, and always being there, even more times than some felt you needed or should be, and even when I was not there for myself or did not know how to. You are one of the greatest men on the other side of paradise above. I pray that God continues to use you to be for others who he needs and ordains you to be.

Last but never least, I thank each of you who stayed up with me throughout the years to be my audience, rather in person or over the phone. Some of you I only know through social media, but you have impacted my life in ways that you have no clue about. It is so easy often for us to motivate others, but not so easy for us to motivate ourselves, and all of you have been something powerful for me in my life and this journey to finally releasing my first book. This assignment continues my healing and self-renewal journey, but even greater, it was created to create the journey for healing and renewal for so many others. The purpose is greater than self. So, I say thank you to everyone for your continued support and I hope you all enjoy the book. Look out for the Audible Version of "Voiceless Voices", Late Summer 2022, which will be narrated by me for a more personal feel.

Social Media

instagram.com/author_khalilahp

www.facebook.com/khalilahpurnell

www.linkedin.com/in/khalilahpurnell

Please sign up for my newsletter and receive a FREE GIFT. Thank you for your support.

www.khalilahhpurnell.com

Also checkout the "Self-Renewed" Journal, now available.

Lightning Source UK Ltd.
Milton Keynes UK
UKHW010942270722
406450UK00002B/316